2019

WORKERS'

COMPENSATION

ALMANAC

Prepared by

APPLIED UNDERWRITERS, INC.

This Almanac is for information and entertainment purposes only. While the information as compiled is believed to be accurate, it should not be relied upon to apply for or underwrite workers' compensation insurance.

Volume Six

Produced Annually Since 2014

Applied Underwriters, SolutionOne, EquityComp, and JumboGC are registered trademarks of Applied Underwriters, Inc., a Berkshire Hathaway company. Rated A+ (Superior) by A.M. Best. Insurance plans protected U.S. Patent No. 7,908,157.

THIS BOOK BELONGS TO:

. . . .

Name

. . . .

Title

. . . .

Contact

Your

QUINTESSENTIAL

GUIDE

to

EVERYTHING WORTH

INVESTIGATING

in

THE WORLD OF

WORKERS'

COMPENSATION

Absolutely Fascinating!

The Workers' Compensation Almanac

is prepared by Applied Underwriters® each year.

This sixth volume is a compendium of workers' compensation information to help keep you informed year-round.

Peruse our articles on current topics to learn about the latest court decisions when it comes to general liability claims in Florida. Read about the eye-opening role fatigue plays in workplace accidents. You'll find an astonishing abundance of charts and tables to educate and inform both you and your clients. Need an electronic copy of this year's Almanac? Visit our Agent portal at **bigdoghq.com** to download a copy.

We wrote the book on Workers' Compensation.™

TABLE OF CONTENTS

LIST OF MONOLINE WORKERS' COMPENSATION CARRIERS BY RATING
(Complete list as of 8/17/2018)

Insurance Group	Best's Rating	Financial Size Category	
North American Casualty Group (Applied Underwriters)	A+	XI	*($750 Million to $1.00 Billion)*
A.I.M. Mutual Insurance Companies	A	VIII	*($100 Million to $250 Million)*
Amerisafe Insurance Group	A	IX	*($250 Million to $500 Million)*
Charter Insurance Group	A	VII	*($50 Million to $100 Million)*
Eastern Alliance Insurance Group	A	VIII	*($100 Million to $250 Million)*
Hawaii Employers' Mutual Insurance Company, Inc.	A	VIII	*($100 Million to $250 Million)*
Lackawanna Insurance Group	A	VII	*($50 Million to $100 Million)*
Lion Insurance Company	A	VIII	*($100 Million to $250 Million)*
Louisiana Workers' Compensation Corporation	A	XII	*($1.00 Billion to $1.25 Billion)*
MEMIC Group	A	IX	*($250 Million to $500 Million)*
New Jersey Casualty Insurance Company	A	IX	*($250 Million to $500 Million)*
Republic and Summit Insurance Pool	A	X	*($500 Million to $750 Million)*
Texas Mutual Insurance Company	A	XV	*($2.00 Billion or greater)*
Workers' Compensation Fund Insurance Group	A	XI	*($750 Million to $1.00 Billion)*
Zenith National Insurance Group	A	X	*($500 Million to $750 Million)*
Accident Fund Group	A-	XII	*($1.00 Billion to $1.25 Billion)*
AmFed Insurance Group	A-	VI	*($25 Million to $50 Million)*
Arrow Mutual Liability Insurance Company	A-	VI	*($25 Million to $50 Million)*
Chesapeake Employers' Insurance Company	A-	X	*($500 Million to $750 Million)*
CopperPoint Mutual Group	A-	XIII	*($1.25 Billion to $1.50 Billion)*
Dakota Group	A-	VII	*($50 Million to $100 Million)*
Employers Insurance Group	A-	XI	*($750 Million to $1.00 Billion)*
FFVA Mutual Insurance Company	A-	VIII	*($100 Million to $250 Million)*
ICW Pool	A-	XII	*($1.00 Billion to $1.25 Billion)*
Kentucky Employers' Mutual Insurance	A-	VIII	*($100 Million to $250 Million)*
LUBA Insurance Group	A-	VII	*($50 Million to $100 Million)*
Midwest Builders' Casualty Group	A-	VII	*($50 Million to $100 Million)*
Missouri Employers Mutual Insurance Company	A-	VIII	*($100 Million to $250 Million)*
New Mexico Mutual Group	A-	VIII	*($100 Million to $250 Million)*

LIST OF MONOLINE WORKERS' COMPENSATION CARRIERS BY RATING
(Complete list as of 8/17/2018) (continued)

Insurance Group	Best's Rating	Financial Size Category	
Pacific Compensation Insurance Company	A-	VIII	($100 Million to $250 Million)
Pinnacol Assurance	A-	XIII	($1.25 Billion to $1.50 Billion)
Retailers Casualty Insurance Company	A-	VI	($25 Million to $50 Million)
FHM Insurance Company	B++	VI	($25 Million to $50 Million)
Fire Districts Insurance Group	B++	VI	($25 Million to $50 Million)
Forestry Mutual Insurance Company	B++	VI	($25 Million to $50 Million)
RetailFirst Insurance Group	B++	VIII	($100 Million to $250 Million)
Stonetrust Commercial Insurance Company	B++	VII	($50 Million to $100 Million)

Note: "Monoline Workers' Compensation Carriers" are defined as at least 90% premium in workers' compensation rounded to 1%.

"On the other hand, he's never had a workplace injury."

WORKPLACE ACCIDENTS: IT'S ABOUT TIME

You'd expect that at the end of the day, when workers are tired and ready to go home, dull responsiveness might make injuries likely. In fact, the most biting time of day for accidents is just before lunch, according to a study done by Pinnacol Assurance, issued on Labor Day 2018.

Construction workers are most vulnerable to getting hurt in the late morning, researchers found. The causes are many and often specific to the worker; a dip in blood sugar, inadequate hydrating, or a faulty breakfast menu are common culprits, the study holds.

In addition to the slow trudge in "metabolic valley" at that hour, more generally, the study found that inexperience is a contributor to workplace injuries: About 44 percent of the injury claims made by construction and natural resource workers happen to those in the first year on the job; 38 percent for healthcare workers; and 30 percent for professional and clerical workers.

Subjecting new hires to a regular workload on day one could be dangerous — especially before noon.

WORKERS' COMPENSATION MEDICATION PRESCRIBING DOWN

The prescribing of medication in workers' compensation cases is down, reportedly, including a 65.1 percent drop in the costs for compounded medications, according to an industry report quoted in Business Insurance this past August.

- Prescription costs per claim were down 10.9 percent in 2017 and overall use of prescribed medicine dipped 8 percent.

- Opioid costs per claim were down 17.3 percent and prescribed opioid use dipped 13.2 percent.

- Compound costs per claim dropped 65.1 percent and use declined 67.3 percent.

Some ascribe the results to better claims management, others to innovations such as in-house pharmacy and prescription monitoring, such as that implemented by Applied Underwriters' in-house pharmacy system.

Regardless, the trend is a good sign.

"And now I will attempt the same feat but without insurance."

SCHEDULE RATING LIMITS BY STATE
Range of Modification (Credit to Debit) (as of 7/1/2017)

State	Maximum Modification	Eligibility *(Min. Annual Premium at Manual Rates)*	Premises	Classification Peculiarities	Medical Facilities
Alabama	25%	$1,000	-10% to +10%	-10% to +10%	-5% to +5%
Alaska		carrier may file			
Arizona	25%	*			
Arkansas	25%				
California		carrier may file			
Colorado	25%	*	-10% to +10%	-10% to +10%	-5% to +5%
Connecticut	25%	$5,500	-10% to +10%	-10% to +10%	-5% to +5%
Delaware		carrier may file			
District of Columbia	25%	*	-10% to +10%	-10% to +10%	-5% to +5%
Florida		not available			
Georgia		carrier may file			
Hawaii		not available			
Idaho	25%	‡	-5% to +5%	-5% to +5%	-5% to +5%
Illinois		carrier may file			
Indiana	50%	Any risk	-10% to +10%	-10% to +10%	-10% to +10%
Iowa	15%	Any risk	-5% to +5%	-5% to +5%	-5% to +5%
Kansas	25%	Any risk	-10% to +10%	-10% to +10%	-5% to +5%
Kentucky	25%	*	-10% to +10%	-10% to +10%	-5% to +5%
Louisiana	25%				
Maine	25%				
Maryland	25%	*	-10% to +10%	-10% to +10%	-5% to +5%
Massachusetts		carrier may file			
Michigan		carrier may file			
Minnesota		carrier may file			
Mississippi	25%	*	-10% to +10%	-10% to +10%	-5% to +5%

SCHEDULE RATING LIMITS BY STATE
Range of Modification (Credit to Debit) (as of 7/1/2017) (continued)

State	Safety Devices	Employees — Selection, Training, Supervision	Management — Cooperation With Insurance Carrier	Management — Safety Organization
Alabama	-5% to +5%	-10% to +10%	-5% to +5%	-5% to +5%
Alaska	carrier may file			
Arizona				
Arkansas				
California	carrier may file			
Colorado	-5% to +5%	-10% to +10%	-5% to +5%	-5% to +5%
Connecticut	-5% to +5%	-10% to +10%	-5% to +5%	-5% to +5%
Delaware	carrier may file			
District of Columbia	-5% to +5%	-10% to +10%	-5% to +5%	-5% to +5%
Florida	not available			
Georgia	carrier may file			
Hawaii	not available			
Idaho	-5% to +5%	-5% to +5%	-5% to +5%	-5% to +5%
Illinois	carrier may file			
Indiana	-10% to +10%	-10% to +10%	-5% to +5%	-5% to +5%
Iowa	-5% to +5%	-5% to +5%	-5% to +5%	-5% to +5%
Kansas	-5% to +5%	-10% to +10%	-5% to +5%	-5% to +5%
Kentucky	-5% to +5%	-10% to +10%	-5% to +5%	-5% to +5%
Louisiana				
Maine				
Maryland	-5% to +5%	-10% to +10%	-5% to +5%	-5% to +5%
Massachusetts	carrier may file			
Michigan	carrier may file			
Minnesota	carrier may file			
Mississippi	-5% to +5%	-10% to +10%	-5% to +5%	-5% to +5%

SCHEDULE RATING LIMITS BY STATE
Range of Modification (Credit to Debit) (as of 7/1/2017) (continued)

State	Maximum Modification	Eligibility (Min. Annual Premium at Manual Rates)	Premises	Classification Peculiarities	Medical Facilities
Missouri		carrier may file			
Montana	25%	Any risk	-10% to +10%	-10% to +10%	-5% to +5%
Nebraska		carrier may file			
Nevada	25%	$500	-10% to +10%	-10% to +10%	-5% to +5%
New Hampshire	25%	$1,000			
New Jersey	25%				
New Mexico	15%	$1,500	-6% to +6%	-6% to +6%	-3% to +3%
New York	5%	$2,500	-2% to 2%	-2% to 2%	-2% to +2%
North Carolina	25%	$2,500	-5% to +5%	-5% to +5%	-10% to +10%
Oklahoma	25%	†	-10% to +10%	-10% to +10%	-5% to +5%
Oregon		not available			
Pennsylvania	25%	Any risk	-10% to +10%	-10% to +10%	-5% to +5%
Rhode Island	25%	*	-10% to +10%	-10% to +10%	-5% to +5%
South Carolina	25%	Any risk	-10% to +10%	-10% to +10%	-5% to +5%
South Dakota	25%	‡	-10% to +10%	-10% to +10%	-5% to +5%
Tennessee	25%	Any risk	-10% to +10%	-10% to +10%	-5% to +5%
Texas	40%	‡			
Utah	25%	$3,500	-10% to +10%	-10% to +10%	-5% to +5%
Vermont	25%	‡	-10% to +10%	-10% to +10%	-5% to +5%
Virginia	15%		-5% to +5%	-5% to +5%	-5% to +5%
West Virginia	25%	$5,000	-10% to +10%	-10% to +10%	-5% to +5%
Wisconsin		not available			

SCHEDULE RATING LIMITS BY STATE
Range of Modification (Credit to Debit) (as of 7/1/2017) (continued)

State	Safety Devices	Employees — Selection, Training, Supervision	Management — Cooperation With Insurance Carrier	Management — Safety Organization
Missouri	carrier may file			
Montana	-5% to +5%	-10% to +10%	-5% to +5%	-5% to +5%
Nebraska	carrier may file			
Nevada	-5% to +5%	-10% to +10%	-5% to +5%	-5% to +5%
New Hampshire				-25% to +25%
New Jersey				
New Mexico	-3% to +3%	-6% to +6%	-3% to +3%	-3% to +3%
New York	-2% to 2%	-2% to 2%	-2% to 2%	-2% to 2%
North Carolina	-10% to +10%	-5% to +5%	-10% to +10%	-5% to +5%
Oklahoma	-5% to +5%	-10% to +10%	-5% to +5%	-5% to +5%
Oregon	not available			
Pennsylvania	-5% to +5%	-10% to +10%	-5% to +5%	-5% to +5%
Rhode Island	-5% to +5%	-10% to +10%	-5% to +5%	-5% to +5%
South Carolina	-5% to +5%	-10% to +10%	-5% to +5%	-5% to +5%
South Dakota	-5% to +5%	-10% to +10%	-5% to +5%	-5% to +5%
Tennessee	-5% to +5%	-10% to +10%	-5% to +5%	-5% to +5%
Texas				
Utah	-5% to +5%	-10% to +10%	-5% to +5%	-5% to +5%
Vermont	-5% to +5%	-10% to +10%	-5% to +5%	-5% to +5%
Virginia	-5% to +5%	-5% to +5%	-5% to +5%	-5% to +5%
West Virginia	-5% to +5%	-10% to +10%	-5% to +5%	-5% to +5%
Wisconsin	not available			

* Annual manual premium must be at least the applicable state minimum eligibility amount shown in Column B of the State Table of Subject Premium Eligibility Amounts. The applicable minimum eligibility amount is the value in effect as of the policy's effective date. Refer to NCCI's Experience Rating Plan Manual Rule 2-A-2 for the State Table of Subject Premium Eligibility Amounts.

‡ Risks that generate premium in excess of the classification minimum premium.

† Risks that generate premium in excess of the classification minimum premium in the private carrier market.

NOTE: These are bureau-filed schedule rating plans. Carriers may file individual schedule rating plans in some states.

Expect big things in workers' compensation. Most classes approved, nationwide. It pays to get a quote from Applied.®
For information call (877) 234-4450 or visit auw.com/us. Follow us at bigdoghq.com.

ANAGRAMS

An anagram is a word or phrase that is made by rearranging all the letters of another word or phrase. For your puzzle-solving pleasure, the following words are anagrams of common workers' compensation insurance-related terms. Solutions are on page 128. Got one for us to solve? Email it to bigdoghq@auw.com. If you stump us, we'll send you a Big Dog bobble head.

Example: UNPRIMED MENU EAR = **UNEARNED PREMIUM**

1. EAGLE EYE WAVER GAWK

2. DEBIT INTENSIFY MEN

3. FOREFRONT SPIRIT JURY

4. BOTANICAL FIVE NOTES

5. ADVISE SOUL SHORTLY

6. IMPROVIDENT DECAL WORKER

7. PORTLY MICE

8. GET PENNANT INDEED

9. AC/DC METAL EPIC

10. LEASED COLD

DIRECT WRITTEN WORKERS' COMPENSATION PREMIUM
IN THE CONTINENTAL UNITED STATES
A Visual Representation by State (as of 9/20/2018)

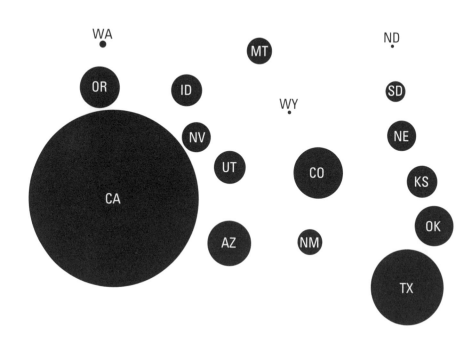

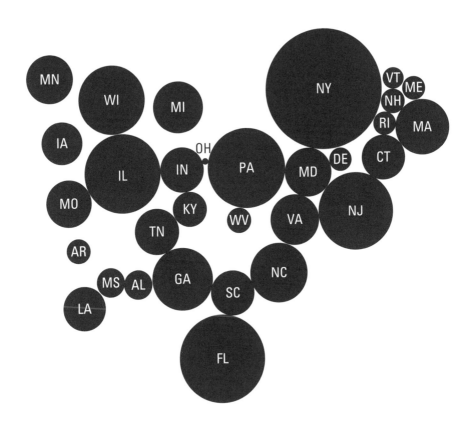

WORKERS' COMPENSATION PRESSURES LOOM: FITCH REPORT

While the U.S. workers' compensation sector had a strong year of underwriting performance in 2017, weaker underwriting results lie ahead, according to the Fitch Ratings: U.S. Workers' Compensation Market Update (Standout Performer in Commercial Lines), released August 2018.

The U.S. commercial lines insurance market experienced "considerable" underwriting losses in 2017, largely due to higher property losses from natural catastrophes and continued weak auto-market results. According to the report, workers' compensation was "the one bright spot," with direct written premium volume of $56 billion in 2017.

The workers' compensation sector had a combined ratio of 92.3 percent in 2017, an improvement from the 95.6 percent 2016 combined ratio, according to the report. The sector's combined ratio improved by more than 10 points over the past five years.

" Fitch believes that workers' compensation will experience some erosion in results going forward. "

But "pricing pressure will continue going forward, though near-term premium volume will likely benefit from exposure growth as employee payrolls are expanding from higher wages and employment in a period of moderately improving economic growth," the report stated. "Fitch believes that workers' compensation will experience some erosion in results going forward, but is still in a position to generate underwriting profits in 2018 and move towards a break-even combined ratio in 2019. Projecting future results is very difficult given historical segment volatility."

The National Council on Compensation Insurance (NCCI) reported that claims frequency moved downward favorably by 6.0 percent in accident year 2017 and 6.2 percent in 2016.

Both indemnity and medical claims severity were relatively stable, compared with historical norms for nearly a decade, but ticked up recently, with NCCI reporting that indemnity claims' severity increased by 4.0 percent in 2017 and 2.7 percent in the previous year.

INDEMNITY CLAIMS PER 1,000 EMPLOYEES BY STATE

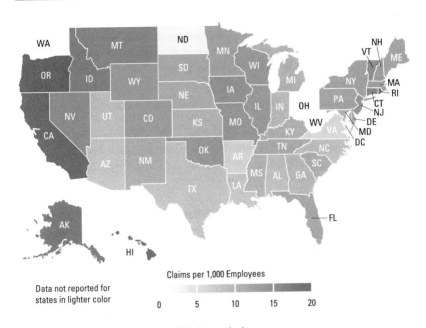

Claims per 1,000 Employees

Data not reported for
states in lighter color

0   5   10   15   20

NCCI 2017 Annual Statistics Bulletin for policy year 2013 at 1st report level.

IT'S SAFER IN INDY – *Indiana federal statistics show the state hit
an all-time low in 2016 of 3.5 per injuries for every 100 full-time
workers. That's an 8 percent drop from the previous year — and a
nearly 70 percent drop from decades past. The figure counts work-
related injuries that were serious enough to require medical attention
beyond first aid.*

Source: *The Northwest Indiana Times*

DID SOMEONE SAY "WHO NEEDS IT?"

According to a poll conducted by Insureon in 2018, 26 percent of small businesses surveyed do not carry workers' compensation insurance, while an additional 30 percent aren't sure if they are required to provide workers' compensation coverage for their staff. This is puzzling, considering most states do require small businesses with employees to carry this coverage.

More small businesses are employing remote workers, but don't carry the proper insurance to protect them across state lines. Nearly one-fourth (24 percent) of surveyed small businesses employ at least one person outside the state where the business is located, but 30 percent don't purchase separate workers' compensation policies for these out-of-state employees, despite the fact that 74 percent are aware that the state where their remote workers are based requires workers' compensation coverage.

"What do you mean, you don't want any?"

OPIOID PRESCRIPTION COSTS PER INJURED WORKER IN THE U.S.

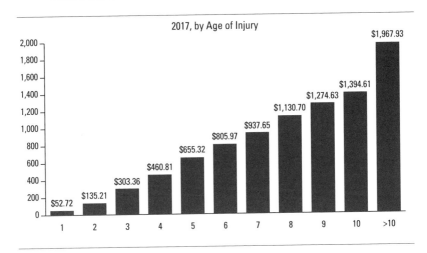

2017, by Age of Injury

Age	Cost
1	$52.72
2	$135.21
3	$303.36
4	$460.81
5	$655.32
6	$805.97
7	$937.65
8	$1,130.70
9	$1,274.63
10	$1,394.61
>10	$1,967.93

PERCENT OF PRESCRIPTIONS ON FORMULARY BY STATE

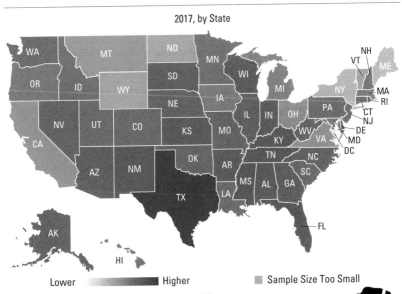

2017, by State

Lower ▬▬▬ Higher   ▮ Sample Size Too Small

CLAIM TYPE DISTRIBUTION BY STATE
Distribution of Risk Counts by Premium Range (as of 9/14/2018)

STATE   Fatal (%)   Perm. Total (%)   Perm. Partial (%)   Temp. Total (%)   Medical Only (%)

CLAIM TYPE DISTRIBUTION BY STATE
Distribution of Risk Counts by Premium Range (as of 9/14/2018) (continued)

STATE — Fatal (%) — Perm. Total (%) — Perm. Partial (%) — Temp. Total (%) — Medical Only (%)

CLAIM TYPE DISTRIBUTION NATIONWIDE
(as of 9/1/2018)

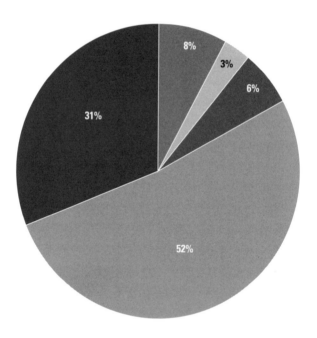

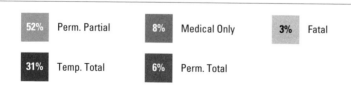

52% Perm. Partial	**8%** Medical Only	**3%** Fatal
31% Temp. Total	**6%** Perm. Total	

CIRCADIAN RHYTHMS AND FATIGUE-RELATED ACCIDENTS

Chris Brogan of AssureNet, creator of so many useful products in telematics and related fields for the effective management of risks related to insuring "wheels," shared a study of circadian rhythms that was conducted by Brian E. O'Neill and Anneke Heitmann, Ph.D. It is believed the results of this study will impact insurers across the board.

Human fatigue is a central concern for the transportation industry, not only because drivers face the challenge of finding time for adequate sleep in their irregular schedules, but also because of the safety-critical nature of the job. Impaired mental capacity due to sleep deprivation, mixed with high demands on alertness and attentiveness, makes for a dangerous combination, one that has been attributed to some $12 billion in yearly costs, and thousands of deaths. Driver fatigue — or more precisely, driver lapses in attention behind the wheel caused by sleep deprivation — has been named one of the leading safety hazards in the transportation industry.

Approaches to reduce fatigue-related accidents include hours-of-service regulations that limit consecutive and cumulative work hours. However, their effectiveness has been compromised, as the incorporation of scientific sleep-wake principles is limited, and little guidance is given to companies and drivers on how to best use these principles to adapt the one-size-fits-all regulation approach to their specific operational conditions. A more effective approach involves a broad evaluation of dispatch and operational practices, to assess the root causes and patterns of fatigue that result in costly — and deadly — accidents.

Such an assessment would empower companies to:

- optimize work schedules
- investigate fatigue-related accidents
- train employees on shiftwork lifestyle management

One approach developed by Circadian Technologies involves the company-wide assessment of driver fatigue and an intervention for its reduction. Specifically, the intervention is a risk-informed, performance-based approach, which allows managers to identify individual work-rest patterns with the highest fatigue risk, and hold managers personally accountable for fatigue risk. The following describes a case study in which Circadian Technologies applied this approach in a major trucking company.

CIRCADIAN RHYTHMS AND FATIGUE-RELATED ACCIDENTS *(continued)*

ASSESSING DRIVER FATIGUE

Driver fatigue was assessed using proprietary analysis software: the Circadian Alertness Simulator (CAS). The software is based on scientific principles of circadian sleep-wake physiology. Individual driver logbook data, covering one month, were processed. Each driver was assigned a cumulative fatigue risk score, in which driver fatigue was ranked on a scale from 0 (no fatigue) to 100 (extreme fatigue), describing the relative risk of accidents due to driver fatigue from any planned sequence of driving and resting hours. The distribution of individual fatigue risk scores within the entire driver population, as well as the group mean for the population, was then analyzed and tracked over consecutive months.

INTERVENTION: RISK-INFORMED, PERFORMANCE-BASED FATIGUE MANAGEMENT

To design an intervention to reduce the risk of driver fatigue, we took into account the fact that driver fatigue in the trucking industry is influenced by several variables, including a) the business that the carrier accepts, b) the sequence of trips constructed by the dispatchers, and c) the day-to-day decisions made by the truck drivers, who alternate work shifts in driving each truck.

"I dreamed I got eight hours of sleep."

CIRCADIAN RHYTHMS AND FATIGUE-RELATED ACCIDENTS *(continued)*

An intervention was designed to reduce the risk of driver fatigue that began with educating dispatchers on how they could reduce fatigue scores by adjusting the timing and duration of daily and weekly work and rest patterns. To achieve that end, some of the techniques included:

- providing rest breaks which allowed two consecutive nights of sleep
- avoiding rapid rotations in the starting time of work
- reducing the number of consecutive shifts worked

Managers and dispatchers in the trucking operation were then provided with monthly analyses of the CAS fatigue risk scores for each driver.

RESULTS

The average fatigue risk scores for the driver population were significantly reduced from 47 to 29 within the first 9 months of the fatigue management intervention [Figure 1]. Also, the percentage of high fatigue risk scores (61 and over) fell from 28.9 percent to 3.9 percent, and the percentage of minimum fatigue risk scores (1-20) increased significantly from 14.9 percent to 44.6 percent.

The reduction in fatigue risk scores was associated with fewer incidences and lower costs of accidents [Figure 2]. The total number of truck accidents dropped 23.5 percent from an average rate of 2.30 per million miles for the three years prior to the intervention to 1.76 per million miles for the first year when fatigue risk score management was instituted. The average cost per accident dropped 65.8 percent from $14,088 to $4,820.

Severity accidents (over $20,000 cost) dropped 55 percent from an average rate of 0.20 per million miles to 0.09 per million miles, and the average cost of severity accidents dropped 66.7 percent from $152,384 per accident to $50,809 per accident over the same time frame. Furthermore, the total cost of loss-of-attention accidents (defined as collisions hitting the rear of another vehicle, loss of control) dropped 80.9 percent from a pre-intervention level of $1,187,699 per year to $226,627 per year.

As a result, the cost of insurance claims to the primary insurer dropped significantly after the implementation of the fatigue management intervention. As shown in Figure 3, the costs of insurance premiums and claims for any given time period tend to have a gap that is largely due to the lag between claims dynamic and premium adjustment. As a result of the program, the loss ratio (insurer losses/gross written premium) dropped from 147 percent to 26 percent.

CIRCADIAN RHYTHMS AND FATIGUE-RELATED ACCIDENTS *(continued)*

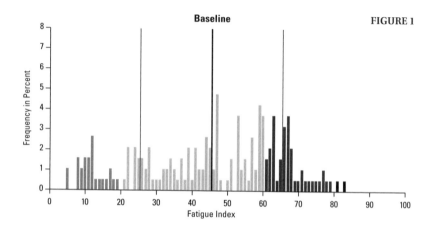

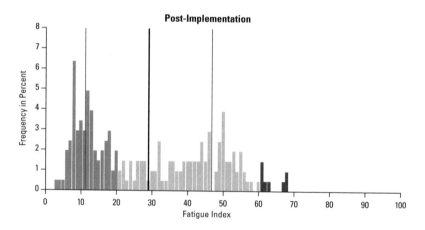

Figure 1: Frequency distribution of fatigue risk scores for individual drivers before (top) and after (bottom) the fatigue management intervention. The fatigue risk score scale (horizontal axis) ranges from 0 (no fatigue) to 100 (extreme fatigue). Fatigue score group averages are indicated by vertical lines. A significant shift towards lower fatigue risk scores was observed after the implementation of the fatigue management intervention.

CIRCADIAN RHYTHMS AND FATIGUE-RELATED ACCIDENTS *(continued)*

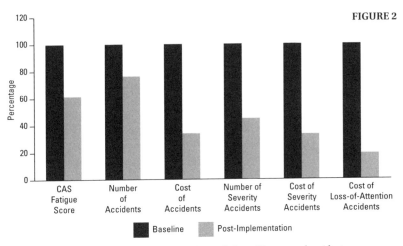

FIGURE 2

Figure 2: Effect of fatigue management intervention on fatigue risk score and accidents. Post-implementation data are shown as percentage of baseline.

FIGURE 3

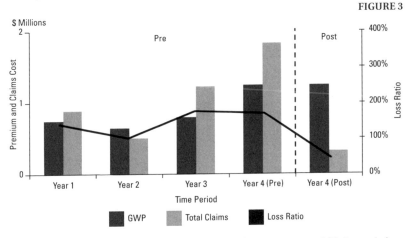

Figure 3: Gross written premium (GWP) and insurer losses (primary insurer only) before and after the fatigue management intervention. The loss ratio dropped from 147 percent to 26 percent as a result of the program.

CONCLUSIONS

Managing by performance-based measure is a well-established method of obtaining tangible results in a business. The key is determining the right performance measure. The most obvious measure might have seemed to be accident rate, but accidents are infrequent events and do not provide a measure of the risk of every driver on a month-to-month basis.

Furthermore, implementing management initiatives based on reduction in accident or injury rates leads to an underreporting of accidents, in part because this encourages managers to devise incentives for employees not to report events or injuries. In contrast, using the fatigue score in a risk-informed, performance-based safety program gives managers and dispatchers incentives to address some of the most important causes of driver fatigue, and, therefore, fatigue-related highway accidents. This approach to fatigue minimization enables managers and dispatchers to make safety-conscious operational decisions, while having sufficient flexibility to balance specific business needs of the operation to stay competitive.

WORKERS' COMPENSATION AVERAGE MEDICAL COST PER LOST-TIME CLAIM

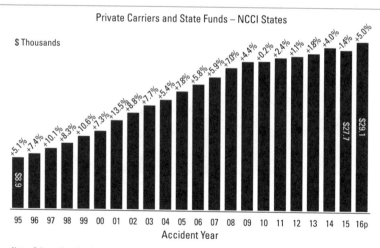

Note: Drivers of workers' compensation medical costs per claim include provider network fees, fee schedules, prescribed medication, hospital costs, new medical treatments, and Medicare set-asides.
p: Preliminary based on data valued as of 12/31/2016.

WORD SEARCH PUZZLE

See if you can find these 17 workers' compensation insurance terms. Solution on page 127.

```
C   D   E   O   P   K   T   R   R   A   C   D   C   R   E
O   F   G   J   V   C   S   A   I   I   Z   I   O   A   T
V   D   A   E   U   E   T   I   M   S   H   S   D   H   A
E   T   R   C   M   I   R   E   R   E   K   A   E   N   R
R   L   E   O   N   P   D   E   Y   I   Q   B   O   M   E
A   V   V   G   C   I   L   Y   X   J   T   I   F   C   S
G   C   O   K   P   A   V   O   L   E   T   L   B   X   A
E   R   C   E   C   K   A   B   Y   A   R   I   U   A   B
R   J   Y   M   I   A   L   C   C   E   Y   T   V   M   H
O   H   T   F   O   R   M   I   A   E   R   Y   I   A   U
H   G   L   A   H   P   F   K   C   B   Q   L   N   O   Y
K   W   A   S   S   I   G   N   E   D   R   I   S   K   N
S   I   U   Z   S   N   O   I   T   A   L   U   G   E   R
S   O   S   S   E   X   P   O   S   U   R   E   C   B   B
A   Z   A   A   M   M   T   A   U   V   F   A   I   B   V
L   L   C   A   P   O   U   F   D   P   R   S   J   Y   S
C   F   T   R   A   Y   X   K   U   U   B   H   A   N   I
```

ACORD
CASUALTY COVERAGE
DISABILITY
EXPOSURE
OVEREXERTION
RISK

ASSIGNED RISK
CLAIM
EMPLOYER
RATING
URAC
BASE RATE

CLASS
COVERAGE
EPIDEMIC
MULTIRISK
REGULATION

INTERESTING WORKERS' COMPENSATION CASES FROM 2018

There are three types of workers' compensation fraud: employer, employee, and healthcare vendor fraud. While employee fraud is the most publicized, it is estimated to represent only about 20 percent of annual workers' compensation fraud, while employer and healthcare fraud costs impact the system on a much larger scale. Below are some of the more interesting workers' compensation fraud cases from 2018.

MONSTER MASHED, PUMPKIN SQUEALED

Thomas Lucey must have thought he was going to have a great Halloween. A trolley operator for Massachusetts Bay Transportation Authority, Lucey, 46, paid a buddy $2,000 to wear a mask and attack him on the job so he could collect workers' compensation benefits. But things didn't go as planned. Wearing a Michael Myers mask and carrying a plastic pumpkin, Lucey's friend showed up at the Cedar Grove trolley station the day before Halloween and beat up Lucey as instructed. He left his pumpkin behind, however, and police took it as evidence when they came to

file a report. Investigators lifted prints from the item and identified them as belonging to Lucey's pal. The man cooperated with police and 18 months later, Lucey was indicted for insurance fraud and a handful of other charges. By then he was already collecting benefits, but MBTA vowed to bring action against him, and his nasty trick is likely to haunt Lucey for many Halloweens to come.

LINEBACKER GETS ADJUSTED

Marcus Buckley was a linebacker for the New York Giants, and Kimberly Jones was an insurance adjuster. Together, they racked up illegal yardage by running claims for fake medical services through the Giants' workers' compensation program. It seems that Buckley had won a legitimate $300,000 settlement for a cumulative trauma claim that he filed in 2006. Apparently impressed with the outcome, he then submitted reimbursement requests under the settlement terms for additional medical services that were never delivered. Jones, meanwhile, played running back by making sure that Pennsylvania Manufacturers Association Insurance Group came through with payment. All told, Buckley and Jones carried off close to $1.6 million from the insurer and from claims handler Gallagher Bassett before

INTERESTING WORKERS' COMPENSATION CASES FROM 2018 *(continued)*

getting sidelined by law enforcement officials. Buckley entered a plea agreement and was sentenced to just 24 months in prison, due to his dementia and Parkinson's disease. Jones, who pleaded guilty for her role in the scheme, was facing up to 20 years in prison. Needless to say, she was sacked.

HELL AND HIGH WATER

When in doubt, go kayaking. That's what government agents decided to do with Deborah Durand, 55, whom they suspected of workers' compensation fraud. Durand, a former U.S. Postal Service employee, had filed for workers' compensation back in 2006, saying she was totally disabled following a back injury. But the Great Falls, MT, resident had restorative back surgery and instead of returning to carrying letters, she hauled nearly $700,000 in benefits to the bank over the next 10 years.

By 2014, federal agents were suspicious, so they posed as marketing representatives and sent Durand a survey asking about her hobbies. Durand returned it, listing camping and kayaking. The agents then told her she'd won a three-day kayaking trip — and they went along with her on the adventure to document it. Agents said they and Durand kayaked four to seven hours each day, with Durand claiming in a follow-up survey that she could manage the trip because she is "fairly strong." During sentencing in U.S. District Court, Durand drew 15 months in prison and an order to pay nearly $1 million in restitution. To be sure, this was one creek Ms. Durand went up without a paddle.

COP CAUGHT, RED-HANDED

Ohio police officer Bryan Eubanks told an impressive tale: He claimed he was shot in the hand during an April 2017 traffic stop that revealed a mobile meth lab in the back of a Geo Tracker. Eubanks even named his assailant, prompting police to launch a statewide search for the suspected vehicle and assailant. Eubanks also filed a claim for workers' compensation benefits after being treated at the local hospital. But his penchant for detail was his downfall, because police soon located the supposed shooter and determined that he was innocent. Then investigators from the Tuscarawas County Sheriff's Office concluded that Eubanks shot himself. Eubanks, 37, and a 14-year veteran of the Newcomerstown, OH, Police Department, pleaded guilty to workers' compensation fraud, forgery, and several

INTERESTING WORKERS' COMPENSATION CASES FROM 2018 *(continued)*

other felony charges and was sentenced to 90 days in jail, ordered to pay $2,500 in fines and $1,973.09 in restitution and was ordered to complete 500 hours of community service. Eubanks was also relieved of his job and his status as an officer of the peace. We can only hope he's now in better hands than his own.

UTICALAND, ICETICA?

Maybe he was just confused. After all, Utica, New York, gets 90 inches of snow a year, and Iceland gets 97 days of annual snowfall. Maybe that's why, when orthopedic surgeon Gregory Shankman filed invoices for workers' compensation medical services he supposedly rendered over 150 days between 2015 and 2017, he claimed that the work was done in his Utica office. But investigators found that Shankman was other places during that time — including vacationing in Iceland.

Investigators said Shankman submitted bills to the New York State Insurance Fund, the County of Oneida, NY, and other insurance organizations, which all paid him nearly $87,000 for services never rendered. He was charged with scheming to defraud, grand larceny, and workers' compensation

fraudulent practices. At sentencing, he was relieved of his medical license and later of $86,896, which he paid in restitution. He was also sentenced to a year's conditional discharge. Wherever he ends up, it won't be Iceland. The judge took his passport.

THAT TAKES BACKBONE

If you're going to commit fraud, go large. Apparently, that's what Michael D. Drobot decided when he built a scheme that bilked the California workers' compensation system out of more than $500 million over 15 years. Between 1997 and 2013, Drobot owned and ran Pacific Hospital of Long Beach. He used a state law, since repealed, that allowed hospitals to pass the costs of device implants performed during spinal surgeries through to workers' compensation insurers. Prosecutors said Drobot bribed a state senator to keep the law in place and paid some $40 million in kickbacks over the years to doctors who referred patients or performed the surgeries. The kickbacks were paid for, prosecutors said, by the sales of medical devices made by International Implants, a California company that Drobot also owned, and which surgeons installed in patients at Pacific Hospital.

Sources didn't disclose how law enforcement agencies got wind of the scheme, but the

INTERESTING WORKERS' COMPENSATION CASES FROM 2018 *(continued)*

FBI, IRS, U.S. Postal Service, and California Department of Insurance were among those investigating. Drobot pleaded guilty to conspiracy and paying illegal kickbacks and was sentenced to more than five years in prison, fined $500,000, and ordered to give back $10 million to government agencies. He was also ordered to sell his Aston Martin, his Porsche, and his Mercedes-Benz.

IT'S ALL IN THE FAMILY

 Attorney Tshombe Anderson of Grand Prairie, TX, had a plan to get rich. But he needed his family's assistance. First, he helped his niece, Lydia Taylor, get an internship with the U.S. Department of Labor. Taylor's role was to dig through workers' compensation claims and lift information about patients' medical conditions and claims statuses. Next, Anderson and his sister, Lydia Bankhead, created two companies to submit fake claims to the Department of Labor – Office of Workers' Compensation Program, using the information Taylor provided.

Anderson's wife and sister-in-law also got involved, news sources said, and even Anderson's mother was asked to participate.

Apparently, they all worked well together, because in just over four years, the family collected a whopping $26 million in payments from the Department of Labor. But Anderson got careless, billing for duplicate medical equipment that was rejected by the claimants whose names he was using. He also billed for medical equipment that was inappropriate for the patients and their conditions, investigators said.

When federal agents raided Anderson's house, they discovered nearly $300,000 in cash, neatly packed for travel. They also found more than $8 million stashed in 25 different bank accounts and another $75,000 in cash. Anderson pleaded guilty to conspiracy to commit healthcare fraud and was sentenced to 10 years in prison. He was also ordered to pay $26.5 million in restitution. All family members except Anderson's 84-year-old mother were charged for their roles in the scam and all pleaded guilty.

CAUGHT DOING THE HEAVY LIFTING

 Matthew Tobolsky, 40, of San Diego, CA, loved going to the gym, where he was frequently seen lifting

INTERESTING WORKERS' COMPENSATION CASES FROM 2018 *(continued)*

heavy weights. Problem was, Tobolsky, a former sheriff's deputy, was supposed to be off work on disability, having filed a workers' compensation claim for a "debilitating back injury" he experienced after lifting two 5-gallon jugs of water at work.

Investigators filmed Tobolsky working out, and he was caught on camera hoisting 80-pound dumbbells in each hand, leg-pressing a whopping 600 pounds, and dead-lifting 315 pounds from the floor to his hips. He was charged with 14 counts of insurance fraud, having collected $46,000 in workers' compensation payments. Authorities estimated that Tobolsky's exploits had caused the system $57,000 in losses. A judge sentenced him to six months of work furlough and three years of probation.

JOYRIDE TO CELLBLOCK H

Tammy Pena had a job to do, but instead she took the low road. She took a client's new Mercedes SUV from her husband's Nanuet, NY, window-tinting shop for a little joy ride. But somehow Pena ran off the road and into a tree, smashing up herself as well as her ride.

What to do? File a workers' compensation claim, of course. Pena said in her claim that she crashed the car and sustained her injuries after picking it up for service. The lies didn't stop there, however. Pena's husband filed additional paperwork with the New York Workers' Compensation Board supporting his wife's claim, falsifying about her wages, and applying for reimbursement.

Forty-five thousand dollars in fraudulent medical bills and indemnity payments later, investigators deduced that Tammy had been out joy-riding when she literally risked life and limb. Pena, 46, and her husband, were both charged with grand larceny, insurance fraud, and other felonies. Tammy was also charged with a misdemeanor.

WHAT'S IN A NAME?

Most employers would be concerned if their employees were injured on the job, and would take steps to make their workplace safer. Not Troy Carson. Carson, 55, owner of Security Code 3, Inc., of San Jose, CA, simply formed a new company to get out of paying higher workers' compensation rates.

But insurers got suspicious after an investigation into how the new company, with the catchy name SC3 DVBE Security Services,

INTERESTING WORKERS' COMPENSATION CASES FROM 2018 *(continued)*

Inc., reported and handled employee injuries. It seems that workers were being pressured not to report injuries they suffered on the job. Investigators said Carson also fudged the amount of payroll and the number of employees at his new enterprise, in order to pay lower workers' compensation premiums. Carson was charged with underreporting payroll by more than $12 million and defrauding his insurer out of some $3.2 million in premiums. But he didn't act alone. Two of his managers were also charged for their roles in the scam, as was their insurance broker. Together the group pulled down 18 felony counts of insurance fraud. Perhaps the next venture the quartet launches will be called 4Cons4Hire.

DIRECT WRITTEN WORKERS' COMPENSATION PREMIUM BY STATE BY YEAR
(IN $MMs) *(as of 8/17/2018)*

State	Year 2017	Year 2016	Year 2015	Year 2014	Year 2013
Alabama	$352	$361	$349	$331	$313
Alaska	$251	$268	$282	$283	$294
Arizona	$843	$859	$842	$818	$761
Arkansas	$254	$249	$260	$253	$265
California	$12,766	$12,961	$12,334	$11,419	$10,293
Colorado	$1,077	$1,065	$1,057	$956	$814
Connecticut	$818	$873	$892	$868	$818
Delaware	$222	$206	$197	$188	$178
District of Columbia	$176	$158	$198	$158	$163
Florida	$3,183	$2,769	$2,625	$2,537	$2,297
Georgia	$1,604	$1,525	$1,447	$1,349	$1,235
Hawaii	$280	$279	$262	$243	$217
Idaho	$417	$391	$368	$343	$324
Illinois	$2,565	$2,720	$2,827	$2,754	$2,685
Indiana	$826	$876	$890	$848	$830
Iowa	$747	$763	$770	$749	$725
Kansas	$413	$435	$474	$493	$477
Kentucky	$504	$508	$513	$514	$491
Louisiana	$798	$814	$834	$869	$812
Maine	$228	$224	$221	$208	$204
Maryland	$963	$980	$963	$931	$890
Massachusetts	$1,256	$1,223	$1,151	$1,081	$1,029
Michigan	$1,097	$1,150	$1,197	$1,194	$1,141
Minnesota	$970	$1,036	$999	$925	$880
Mississippi	$354	$354	$361	$379	$326
Missouri	$921	$934	$924	$896	$826

DIRECT WRITTEN WORKERS' COMPENSATION PREMIUM BY STATE BY YEAR
(IN $MMs) *(as of 8/17/2018)* *(continued)*

State	Year 2017	Year 2016	Year 2015	Year 2014	Year 2013
Montana	$288	$287	$287	$284	$276
Nebraska	$376	$385	$389	$382	$370
Nevada	$363	$371	$364	$344	$309
New Hampshire	$243	$259	$265	$271	$265
New Jersey	$2,443	$2,495	$2,435	$2,385	$2,210
New Mexico	$269	$269	$296	$291	$273
New York	$5,943	$5,894	$5,524	$5,261	$5,191
North Carolina	$1,448	$1,493	$1,488	$1,431	$1,356
Oklahoma	$662	$693	$811	$893	$972
Oregon	$708	$707	$679	$664	$645
Pennsylvania	$2,615	$2,669	$2,725	$2,645	$2,619
Rhode Island	$220	$227	$213	$200	$184
South Carolina	$827	$782	$729	$702	$665
South Dakota	$176	$177	$181	$176	$172
Tennessee	$867	$873	$859	$861	$895
Texas	$2,344	$2,365	$2,742	$2,844	$2,674
Utah	$445	$442	$423	$412	$377
Vermont	$190	$200	$197	$185	$175
Virginia	$1,045	$1,021	$981	$926	$887
West Virginia	$259	$262	$323	$319	$337
Wisconsin	$1,960	$2,005	$1,941	$1,804	$1,747

WORKERS' COMPENSATION AGGREGATES AND AVERAGES
(as of March, 2018)

Kinds of Insurance	Year	Direct Premiums Earned (000)	Ratios to Direct Premiums Earned	
			Losses Incurred	Loss Adj Expenses Incurred
Workers' Compensation	2008	46,083,163	62.8	14.1
	2009	39,523,257	65.9	15.6
	2010	39,547,796	73.3	16.3
	2011	42,541,429	68.5	16.2
	2012	44,496,603	66.3	13.8
	2013	48,475,896	62.6	13.7
	2014	51,692,304	59.7	13.6
	2015	56,618,238	57.3	13.3
	2016	58,020,405	54.5	13.6
	2017	55,564,858	49.9	13.8
Totals		**482,563,949**	**61.3**	**14.3**

SAFETY MOTIVATOR – *On January 3, 2018, the U.S. Occupational Safety and Health Administration adjusted its civil penalties for workplace safety violations to account for inflation. The penalty for willful and repeat violations increased from $126,749 to $129,336. The fines for other-than-serious, serious, and failure to abate violations rose from $12,615 to $12,934 per violation.*

Source: Business Insurance

WORKERS' COMPENSATION AGGREGATES AND AVERAGES
(as of March, 2018) (continued)

		Ratios to Direct Premiums Written			
Kinds of Insurance	Year	Comms & Brokerage Incurred	Other Underwriting Expense Incurred	Dividends to Policyholders	Combined Ratio After Div
Workers' Compensation	2008	7.6	16.2	2.9	103.6
	2009	8.0	16.2	3.5	109.1
	2010	8.0	17.9	2.5	117.9
	2011	8.1	17.5	2.5	112.7
	2012	8.4	16.8	2.3	107.6
	2013	8.4	16.1	2.0	102.7
	2014	8.4	14.5	1.9	98.0
	2015	8.4	14.4	2.3	95.7
	2016	8.6	14.6	3.0	94.3
	2017	9.2	15.0	2.3	90.1
Totals		8.3	15.8	2.5	102.1

YOU MAY WANT TO CHECK – *A 2018 study conducted by the American College of Occupational and Environmental Medicine (ACOEM) found that of the 700 employers they studied, 80 percent offered some type of workplace health promotion program.*
In contrast, only 45 percent of those workers reported awareness of a workplace wellness program. Of employees who had access to wellness programs, 55 percent took advantage of the benefit.

Source: American College of Occupational and Environmental Medicine

PTSD CLAIMS EMERGE IN NEW WORKPLACE ENVIRONMENTS

Post-traumatic stress disorder (PTSD) is variously defined and described, as it is an imprecise, emerging area of concentration. To be covered by workers' compensation, PTSD victims need to meet the criteria set out in the American Psychiatric Association's Diagnostic and Statistical Manual of Mental Disorders (DSM-5), and be diagnosed by a licensed psychologist or psychiatrist. Broadly, PTSD symptoms usually start a month or more after the incident; acute stress disorder is used to describe PTSD lasting under a month.

States cover PTSD variously in their workers' compensation law, depending upon whether or not the state recognizes that event as a work injury. If the event that led to the PTSD condition was physical in nature, most states recognize it as a mental injury caused by a physical injury, and therefore compensable. If the claimant was involved in a traumatic incident, without physical injury, some states may not recognize the PTSD claim.

When filing a claim under workers' compensation for PTSD, only first responders have a generally direct way of getting benefits. Yet, according to that same DSM-5, symptoms spearing after an exposure to death (real or threatened), grave injury, or sexual violence may be deemed workplace related and thus result in a PTSD claim.

To the customary list of safety officers, firefighters, and emergency medical staff, we may now add school personnel witnessing shootings or violent actions, and a host of other situational, on-the-job traumas that the claimant may re-experience as upsetting memories, bad dreams, flashbacks, and physical reactions, or associations related to the original event. Other complications may follow or be included.

As mass shootings in the workplace take their toll, legislators are loosening the restrictions on workers' compensation claims for PTSD, especially for first responders.

Lawmakers responded to the 2018 Parkland, Florida, mass shootings by allowing workers' compensation disability benefits (not just medical costs) for first responders who developed PTSD after witnessing the events, which they said were marked by "grievous bodily harm of a nature that shocks the conscience" (Fla. S.B. 376 [2018]).

In short, pervasive violence in the workplace is begetting a new set of claimants and an emerging set of rules and standards, all of which will affect rates and coverages. Workers' compensation professionals would do well to read the DSM-5 as the basis for future changes and evolutions of PTSD claims.

DOUBLE TOLL FOR CARPAL TUNNEL

In 2018, the Montana Supreme Court ruled that a Liberty Mutual unit, which covered an injured employee's carpal tunnel syndrome when first diagnosed, was also liable for coverage when the injury later worsened — even though Liberty Mutual was no longer the client's insurer.

According to the ruling in Montana State Fund v. Liberty Northwest Ins. Corp, Kim Wiard began working at Tricon Timber, a Montana-based company in 2002 and was diagnosed with bilateral carpal tunnel syndrome in 2011. Liberty accepted liability for treatment of the occupational disease in August 2011. Ms. Wiard transferred to a different job position at Tricon and her symptoms largely dissipated.

" [The Montana State Fund] denied the claim, asserting the occupational disease diagnosis preceded the fund's insurance coverage. *"*

In 2012 or early 2013, Ms. Wiard switched to another position at Tricon, which she found more mentally and physically demanding than her previous positions, the ruling states. On Nov. 1, 2013, the Montana State Fund became the client's workers' compensation insurer. After working in her new position for a time, Ms. Wiard sought medical treatment for pain in both wrists in February 2014. She was taken off-the-job and scheduled for care. Her condition worsened and, after leaving work, she went to the emergency room complaining of severe right wrist pain radiating into her shoulder. She was diagnosed with acute exacerbation of carpal tunnel syndrome, given medication, and referred to an orthopedic surgeon. Two days later, she underwent an emergency carpal tunnel release on her left wrist, and the following month the same surgeon performed a carpal tunnel release on her right wrist.

Ms. Wiard filed an occupational disease claim for the emergency surgery with the Montana State Fund, which denied the claim, asserting that her occupational disease diagnosis preceded the fund's insurance coverage. Ms. Wiard then submitted her claim to Liberty, who denied liability on the basis that the Fund was liable.

DOUBLE TOLL FOR CARPAL TUNNEL *(continued)*

The Montana State Fund paid Ms. Wiard's benefits and the insurers then filed cross motions for summary judgment on the issue of liability in workers' compensation court (WCC), which granted summary judgment in favor of Liberty. The court concluded that Ms. Wiard's later job duties "materially aggravated her occupational disease."

"There is no dispute here that Wiard is not suffering from a new and different occupational disease," the ruling stated. "She is suffering from a recurrence of the same occupational disease, while working for the same employer. The WCC's determination that Wiard's later work materially aggravated her CTS is insufficient to shift liability from Liberty to State Fund."

© MARK ANDERSON, WWW.ANDERTOONS.COM

"I was making money hand over fist. Then I got carpal tunnel."

HOME VS. OFFICE – *The share of workers doing some or all of their work at home grew from 19 percent in 2003 to 22 percent in 2016. In this same period, the average time employed persons spent working at home increased by 34 minutes (from 2.6 hours to 3.1 hours).*

Source: U.S. Bureau of Labor Statistics

RATES IN INTERESTING CLASS CODES

All states in the U.S. use a classification and rating system. In most cases, these systems are broadly similar to one another. The system is composed of more than 700 governing, or group classifications, each of which represents the normal activities of a particular type of business operation. Without job classification codes, a firm employing clerical workers (Class 8810) might pay the same rate for workers' compensation insurance as a company of trapeze artists (Class 9186).

Most classifications are called Basic Classifications, where it is the business of the employer (the insured) that is classified and not the separate employments, occupations, or operations of individual employees within the business.

However, there are exceptions. Several occupations are common across so many businesses that special classifications have been designed to fit these situations. These are called Standard Exceptions, and include jobs such as clerical office employees, drivers, chauffeurs, and outside salespersons.

Some operations that look very different than the employer's main business, but are a routine part of the business operation, are called General Inclusions. Some examples include employee cafeteria operations or workers who maintain the employer's building.

Some businesses are considered so unusual that they are separately classified, even though they are not a secondary business. General Exclusion examples include employer-operated day care services and aircraft operations, among others.

See the next few pages for rates in different class codes that we find interesting.

MORE SCRIPTS, MORE INDEMNITY – *A 2018 study by the California Workers' Compensation Institute (CWCI) shows the likelihood that indemnity was paid on a workers' compensation claim increased with the number of concurrent prescriptions the injured worker was on. More than half (51.6 percent) of the claims with one to two prescription drugs were indemnity cases versus 91.3 percent of those with five or more concurrent drugs.*

Source: CWCI

RATES IN INTERESTING CLASS CODES
(as of 8/31/2018) (continued)

	Class 0005 Farm: Nursery		Class 0037 Farm: Field Crops		Class 5213 Concrete Constr NOC	
1	Minnesota	8.88	California	11.47	New York	24.27
2	New Jersey	8.16	Maine	9.18	Connecticut	22.15
3	Wisconsin	7.59	Alaska	9.03	Illinois	19.89
4	Delaware	7.49	Oklahoma	8.77	Massachusetts	18.83
5	California	7.44	Louisiana	7.85	New Jersey	18.56
6	Connecticut	7.23	New Mexico	7.70	New Hampshire	17.92
7	Idaho	6.50	New Hampshire	7.54	Rhode Island	16.90
8	Wyoming	6.18	Utah	7.47	Maine	16.48
9	Washington	5.95	New York	7.41	Oklahoma	12.86
10	Missouri	5.91	Connecticut	7.38	Michigan	12.74
11	Pennsylvania	5.82	Arizona	7.35	Iowa	12.04
12	Rhode Island	5.75	Missouri	6.99	Pennsylvania	11.77
13	Florida	5.72	Delaware	6.90	Vermont	11.73
14	Iowa	5.72	Minnesota	6.77	Maryland	11.52
15	Alaska	5.58	Montana	6.64	Wisconsin	11.18
16	Illinois	5.48	Idaho	6.41	Florida	11.02
17	Oklahoma	5.08	Georgia	6.21	District of Columbia	10.69
18	Montana	5.07	Wyoming	6.18	Delaware	10.51
19	Vermont	4.80	Rhode Island	6.16	Nebraska	10.47
20	Hawaii	4.75	South Carolina	6.09	California	10.13
21	Georgia	4.60	Iowa	6.05	North Carolina	10.10
22	Colorado	4.59	Texas	6.02	Washington	9.95
23	Nebraska	4.43	Colorado	5.95	Minnesota	9.32
24	Maine	4.41	Florida	5.93	Nevada	9.31
25	New Hampshire	4.37	Alabama	5.93	Missouri	9.19
26	Michigan	4.37	Washington	5.86	Montana	9.11

RATES IN INTERESTING CLASS CODES
(as of 8/31/2018) (continued)

	Class 0005 Farm: Nursery		Class 0037 Farm: Field Crops		Class 5213 Concrete Constr NOC	
27	New York	4.25	Pennsylvania	5.79	Georgia	8.92
28	Kentucky	4.24	South Dakota	5.74	Idaho	8.90
29	New Mexico	4.13	North Dakota	5.61	Alaska	8.46
30	Arizona	4.06	Maryland	5.35	Tennessee	8.06
31	Nevada	3.95	Tennessee	5.29	South Dakota	7.82
32	South Dakota	3.94	Nebraska	5.21	Louisiana	7.78
33	Alabama	3.92	Vermont	5.17	South Carolina	7.55
34	Louisiana	3.72	Wisconsin	5.14	New Mexico	7.38
35	Ohio	3.64	Mississippi	5.13	Alabama	7.37
36	South Carolina	3.60	West Virginia	5.02	Arizona	6.90
37	North Carolina	3.47	Oregon	4.91	Virginia	6.83
38	Kansas	3.41	Kansas	4.75	Kansas	6.63
39	District of Columbia	3.25	Illinois	4.54	West Virginia	6.57
40	Texas	3.13	District of Columbia	4.48	Utah	6.56
41	Indiana	3.11	Michigan	4.34	Mississippi	6.51
42	Maryland	3.09	Nevada	4.32	Colorado	6.25
43	Oregon	3.07	Kentucky	4.12	Texas	5.90
44	Tennessee	3.06	Virginia	3.73	Ohio	5.66
45	Utah	2.92	Indiana	3.59	Oregon	5.29
46	Massachusetts	2.88	Ohio	3.55	Arkansas	5.29
47	Virginia	2.65	Hawaii	3.43	Hawaii	5.16
48	Mississippi	2.40	New Jersey	3.33	Kentucky	4.86
49	West Virginia	2.32	Arkansas	2.87	Indiana	4.57
50	Arkansas	2.26	Massachusetts	2.71	North Dakota	4.38
51	North Dakota	1.80	North Dakota	1.78	Wyoming	4.02

RATES IN INTERESTING CLASS CODES
(as of 8/31/2018) (continued)

	Class 5221 Concrete Work Floors		Class 5506 Street/Road Paving		Class 7228 Trucking (Local)	
1	New York	17.37	New York	25.05	New Jersey	19.17
2	Connecticut	13.77	Delaware	16.38	New York	18.26
3	Washington	12.41	California	13.70	Connecticut	15.11
4	New Jersey	11.69	Rhode Island	13.37	California	14.73
5	Alaska	11.47	New Jersey	13.06	Alaska	13.22
6	Illinois	10.43	Connecticut	12.68	Michigan	13.09
7	Montana	10.39	South Carolina	12.25	Washington	12.67
8	California	10.27	Louisiana	12.08	Illinois	12.59
9	Rhode Island	10.17	Oklahoma	11.97	Delaware	12.55
10	Delaware	9.88	Arizona	11.01	Louisiana	12.19
11	Minnesota	9.82	District of Columbia	10.6	Hawaii	11.87
12	Maine	9.77	Illinois	9.96	Vermont	11.38
13	Vermont	9.69	West Virginia	9.72	Ohio	11.23
14	New Hampshire	9.36	New Hampshire	9.69	Iowa	11.10
15	Wisconsin	8.90	New Mexico	9.58	Pennsylvania	10.90
16	Pennsylvania	8.68	Pennsylvania	9.49	North Carolina	10.79
17	Michigan	8.42	Iowa	9.27	Montana	10.24
18	Iowa	8.42	Florida	9.23	Missouri	10.10
19	Missouri	7.31	Hawaii	9.15	Massachusetts	10.10
20	Idaho	7.26	Nebraska	9.00	Rhode Island	10.08
21	Colorado	7.01	Maine	8.77	Maine	9.96
22	Florida	7.01	North Carolina	8.68	Oklahoma	9.87
23	District of Columbia	6.92	Texas	8.59	South Carolina	9.75
24	Massachusetts	6.89	Georgia	8.54	Wisconsin	9.49
25	Louisiana	6.84	South Dakota	8.43	New Hampshire	9.49
26	Maryland	6.81	Kentucky	8.42	Nebraska	9.29

RATES IN INTERESTING CLASS CODES
(as of 8/31/2018) (continued)

	Class 5221 Concrete Work Floors		Class 5506 Street/Road Paving		Class 7228 Trucking (Local)	
27	South Carolina	6.80	Vermont	8.31	Texas	9.06
28	Kansas	6.65	Montana	8.18	Idaho	8.76
29	Oklahoma	6.50	Minnesota	7.99	Georgia	8.67
30	Utah	6.35	Missouri	7.92	New Mexico	8.54
31	Georgia	6.32	Mississippi	7.90	Minnesota	8.47
32	Nebraska	6.30	Michigan	7.83	Alabama	8.42
33	North Carolina	6.18	Wisconsin	7.79	Maryland	8.23
34	South Dakota	6.08	Nevada	7.79	Oregon	8.11
35	Arizona	6.03	Tennessee	7.73	Mississippi	7.66
36	Alabama	5.63	Maryland	7.65	Florida	7.35
37	Oregon	5.61	Massachusetts	7.63	Virginia	7.34
38	Mississippi	5.58	Oregon	7.24	District of Columbia	7.18
39	Tennessee	5.52	Virginia	7.20	Tennessee	7.08
40	Ohio	5.51	Colorado	6.96	Nevada	6.92
41	New Mexico	5.33	Alaska	6.95	Wyoming	6.85
42	Kentucky	5.12	Washington	6.85	Colorado	6.74
43	Virginia	5.10	Alabama	6.80	Arizona	6.50
44	Hawaii	5.06	Idaho	6.68	South Dakota	6.49
45	Texas	5.02	Indiana	5.75	Kansas	6.32
46	North Dakota	4.38	Kansas	5.19	Utah	6.04
47	Arkansas	4.17	Ohio	4.61	North Dakota	5.98
48	Wyoming	4.02	Arkansas	4.37	West Virginia	5.55
49	Nevada	4.00	North Dakota	3.37	Arkansas	4.83
50	Indiana	3.45	Wyoming	2.78	Indiana	4.68
51	West Virginia	3.40	Utah	0.00	Kentucky	3.58

RATES IN INTERESTING CLASS CODES
(as of 8/31/2018) (continued)

	Class 7229 Trucking (Long Dist.)		Class 7380 Chauffeurs NOC	
1	New Jersey	19.17	Connecticut	15.02
2	New York	18.26	New Jersey	15.01
3	Connecticut	16.11	New York	14.72
4	North Carolina	15.83	California	13.12
5	Rhode Island	15.58	Illinois	10.79
6	Maine	15.34	Alaska	10.65
7	California	14.73	Rhode Island	8.81
8	Illinois	14.35	Louisiana	8.24
9	Vermont	14.01	Oklahoma	8.24
10	Alaska	13.22	Minnesota	8.14
11	South Carolina	13.20	Vermont	7.98
12	Michigan	13.09	New Mexico	7.72
13	Missouri	12.84	Maryland	7.09
14	Maryland	12.82	North Carolina	7.04
15	Hawaii	12.59	Montana	6.96
16	Delaware	12.55	Hawaii	6.92
17	Minnesota	12.29	New Hampshire	6.89
18	Washington	12.29	Massachusetts	6.85
19	Louisiana	12.19	Wisconsin	6.84
20	New Mexico	11.44	Washington	6.82
21	Oklahoma	11.39	Maine	6.82
22	Iowa	10.98	Missouri	6.76
23	Wisconsin	10.94	Alabama	6.57
24	Nebraska	10.93	Ohio	6.54
25	Pennsylvania	10.90	Iowa	6.30
26	Montana	10.24	Georgia	6.27

RATES IN INTERESTING CLASS CODES
(as of 8/31/2018) (continued)

	Class 7229 Trucking (Long Dist.)		Class 7380 Chauffeurs NOC	
27	Massachusetts	10.10	South Carolina	6.18
28	Alabama	9.90	Nebraska	6.11
29	Georgia	9.57	Colorado	6.10
30	Kentucky	9.56	Florida	6.10
31	Texas	9.06	Texas	5.95
32	Arizona	9.03	Michigan	5.75
33	Ohio	9.00	Wyoming	5.56
34	Tennessee	8.84	Tennessee	5.52
35	Idaho	8.76	Virginia	5.40
36	Utah	8.75	Kentucky	5.25
37	Colorado	8.70	District of Columbia	5.10
38	Virginia	8.68	Mississippi	4.95
39	Arkansas	8.63	Idaho	4.72
40	South Dakota	8.31	South Dakota	4.62
41	Mississippi	8.29	Kansas	4.58
42	New Hampshire	8.26	Oregon	4.44
43	District of Columbia	8.19	Utah	4.26
44	Oregon	8.11	North Dakota	4.07
45	Nevada	7.85	Indiana	3.62
46	Kansas	7.44	Arkansas	3.42
47	Florida	7.35	West Virginia	3.32
48	Wyoming	6.85	Arizona	0.00
49	West Virginia	6.57	Delaware	0.00
50	Indiana	6.53	Nevada	0.00
51	North Dakota	5.98	Pennsylvania	0.00

RATES IN INTERESTING CLASS CODES
(as of 11/23/2018) (continued)

These heat maps provide an interesting way to look at class code rates on a national basis. States with the darkest colors represent the highest rates, while the light colors represent lower rates. These heat maps are pictorial interpretations of the data found in the Rates in Interesting Class Codes charts, shown on the previous pages.

CLASS 0005: FARM, NURSERY

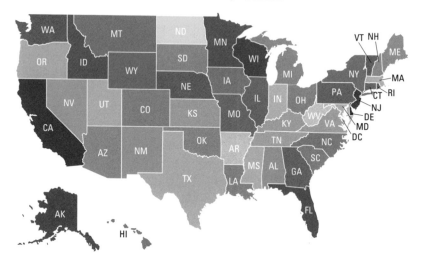

PROGRESSIVE CANNABIS COVERAGE – *California's first filing and approval of an admitted commercial insurer offering insurance for the cannabis industry was announced in November 2017. The first surety bond program for the industry was announced in February 2018, and the first coverage for commercial landlords for the industry was announced in May 2018.*

Source: California Department of Insurance

RATES IN INTERESTING CLASS CODES
(as of 11/23/2018) (continued)

CLASS 0037: FARM FIELD CROPS

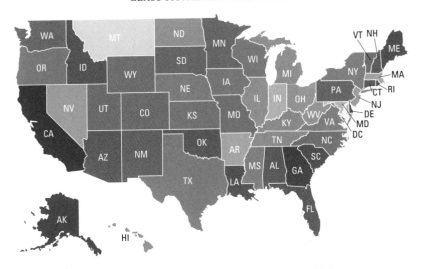

CLASS 5213: CONCRETE CONSTRUCTION – NOC

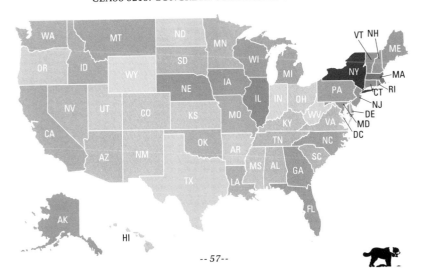

RATES IN INTERESTING CLASS CODES
(as of 11/23/2018) (continued)

CLASS 5506: STREET OR ROAD PAVING

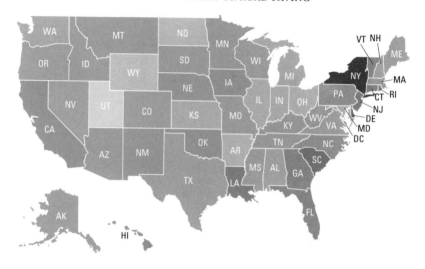

CLASS 5551: ROOFING - ALL KINDS

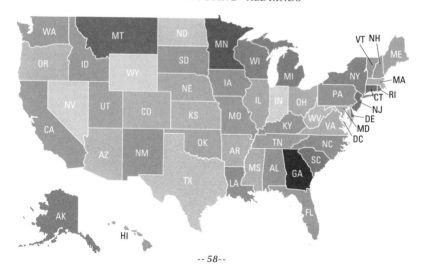

RATES IN INTERESTING CLASS CODES
(as of 11/23/2018) (continued)

CLASS 7228: TRUCKING (LOCAL)

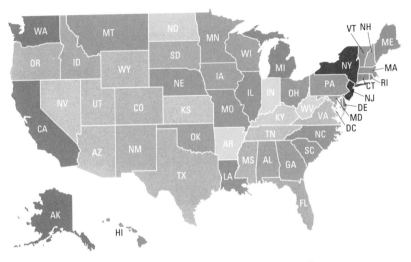

CLASS 7229: TRUCKING (LONG DISTANCE)

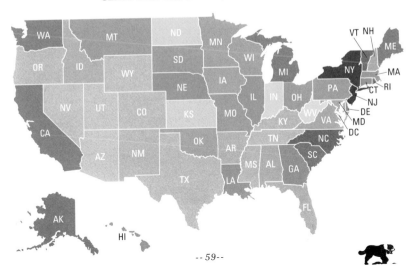

RATES IN INTERESTING CLASS CODES
(as of 11/23/2018) (continued)

CLASS 7380: CHAUFFEURS ~ NOC

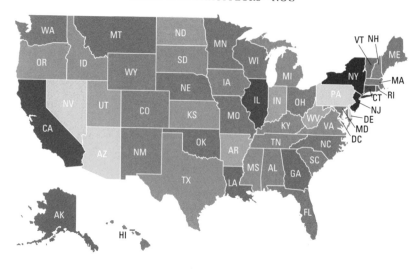

ALLEGED HIGHEST WORKERS' COMPENSATION SETTLEMENT ~

Attorney Christopher Asvar reportedly secured the highest known workers' compensation insurance settlement in U.S. history, totaling $10 million. The case involved an employee who was driving home from work in the early hours of the morning when her vehicle left the road and collided with a tree. She suffered severe trauma, including a life-changing brain injury in the accident.

Source: Northern California Record

INDEPENDENT CONTRACTORS AND WORKERS' COMPENSATION COVERAGE

Generally, workers' compensation insurance covers only employees. A company that hires an independent contractor does not have to purchase workers' compensation coverage for that individual, and this limits the independent contractor's ability to receive workers' compensation benefits. An independent contractor might recover compensation, however, when some form of negligence can be proved or some lapse in safety precaution caused an injury. But the trend is changing.

The Ohio Bureau of Workers' Compensation notes: "Sometimes employers mistakenly consider a worker to be an independent contractor and neglect to provide workers' compensation coverage. If an employer controls the working hours, selection of materials, traveling routes, and quality of performance of a worker, an employer-employee relationship exists and the employer is required to provide workers' compensation coverage for that employee."

This is consistent with last year's California Superior Court decision in Dynamex Operations West where the court made it more difficult to qualify as an independent contractor. The Bureau also notes, "Independent contractors and subcontractors may elect coverage for themselves if they are sole proprietors or partners." Insurance agents would do well to suggest the coverage.

"Now go forth as an independent contractor, keeping a careful diary of your travel expenses."

CROSSWORD PUZZLE

See if you can complete this crossword puzzle in less than 15 minutes. Solution on page 126.

ACROSS

4 The max or total amount of coverage payable for losses during a policy period.

5 Amount insurers set aside to cover claims incurred but not yet paid.

9 Amount of premium used to purchase reinsurance.

11 An association organized to absorb losses through a risk-sharing mechanism.

12 Termination of a policy when client fails to pay required renewal premium.

13 Abbreviation for the group sent in to investigate suspected fraud.

14 An insurer not licensed to do business within a given state.

16 An agent selling insurance of specific insurer.

17 When an insurance company takes legal action against a fraudulent claimant.

18 A ground-up layer of loss retained by a policy holder.

DOWN

1 A person who analyzes probabilities of risk and calculates premiums.

2 Contingencies outlined in an insurance policy.

3 A fund established to compensate a partially disabled employee who sustains another injury.

4 An _____ company accepts risk from a primary insurer or another reinsurer.

6 Value of insured losses expressed as a cost per unit of insurance.

7 Risk of possible loss.

8 ____ time injury.

10 The five-digit ID number assigned by NAIC is the _____ Code.

12 Type of liability that carries a long settlement period.

15 A refund of a portion of the premium paid.

16 Percentage of premium paid to agents by insurance companies.

CROSSWORD PUZZLE *(continued)*

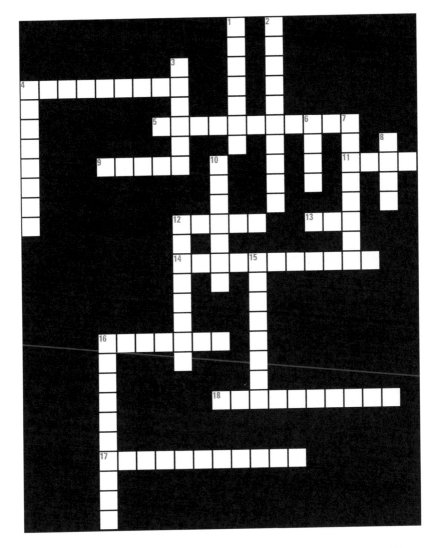

SPOT THE PHONY

Below are three workers' compensation cases. Here's the catch: One is false and the others are true (give or take some non-essential details to make Googling harder.) See if you can determine which cases are legitimate and which case is not. Answer is on page 128.

TAKE A KNEE

Cecilia O'Hare of Wayne, PA, was a 74-year-old nurse with a long history of medical issues with her left leg. Two separate car accidents in 1964 and 1987 severely damaged her left ankle and knee and required screw and side plates in her left femur. In 1988 she slipped and broke the same femur, and in 2000, she fell off a curb, resulting in a broken pelvis. Regardless, O'Hare continued to work as a nurse. In 2005 while delivering medication to a patient, she pivoted to collect a glass of water and heard her leg pop. X-rays showed she'd fractured her left femur, and she filed a workers' compensation claim. Her claim was denied after the workers' compensation commission ruled that the state of her left leg made her susceptible

to a "spontaneous fragility fracture" — an event that could have occurred during any normal activity.

NOT-SO-HAPPY MEAL

Jason Swan, a city utility employee in Winston-Salem, NC, was taking his lunch break in his city-provided work truck. After going through the McDonald's drive-thru and eating his meal in the truck, he decided to enjoy a post-meal cigarette, during which he had a coughing fit. While coughing uncontrollably, Swan stepped out of the truck, tripped, fell, hit his head on the ground, and blacked out. Upon regaining consciousness, he found he had hurt his back so badly he was unable to move. Doctor's medical examinations resulted in work restrictions that made him unable to return to his position, and he filed for workers' compensation. The city denied his claim due to their long-standing policy against workers smoking inside its vehicles.

TOUGH GUY, TOUGH LUCK

Michael Daniels was an operator on the milk-packing machines at a local dairy in Frankfort, KY. While on the machine line in mid-September, the machine malfunctioned

SPOT THE PHONY *(continued)*

and Daniels was hit by nearly a dozen containers of milk. He noticed a red welt on his leg where the containers had made impact. He reportedly felt it was "no big deal" at the time and did not report the injury. The next day, he noticed the welt was bigger and had begun to bruise. By October, he noticed the spot was red and discolored, and had become an open wound. He sought treatment from his family physician who referred him to a specialist, who suggested that due to the extent of the infection, he should seek workers' compensation benefits. He reported the injury on the last day of October. Benefits were denied after it was determined Daniels "failed to report his injury in a timely manner."

"I realize it's part of your job, but I'd like to get your arrow count down."

WORKERS' COMPENSATION STATES BY TYPE
(NCCI, INDEPENDENT, MONOPOLISTIC)

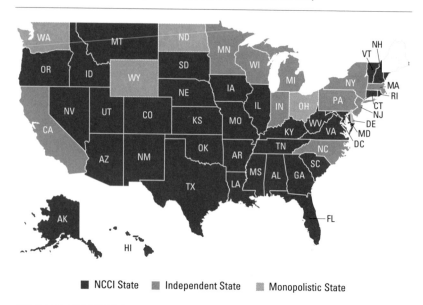

■ NCCI State   ■ Independent State   ■ Monopolistic State

PUFF, THE MAGIC ACTUARY ~ *Replying to calls from regulators in California, insurers have begun to offer workers' compensation programs for the cannabis industry in the Golden State. Part of a "high minded" approach to the societal and legislative trends, insurers will look to cover growers, extractors, manufacturing, packaging, warehousing and distribution, transportation and dispensaries, analytical labs, medicine manufacturers and food and beverage products. Sounds a little like big pharma — because it's getting there.*

The problem of insuring cannabis business grew out of the illicit nature of the business itself. That seems solved, now that cannabis is legal in California — and actuaries should get the credit, together with underwriters, for lighting up a new field for insuring. But of course, note that the Federal government still considers cannabis to be illegal.

Source: Insurance Advocate

DISTRIBUTION OF PREMIUM BY PREMIUM RANGE BY STATE
(as of 9/14/2018)

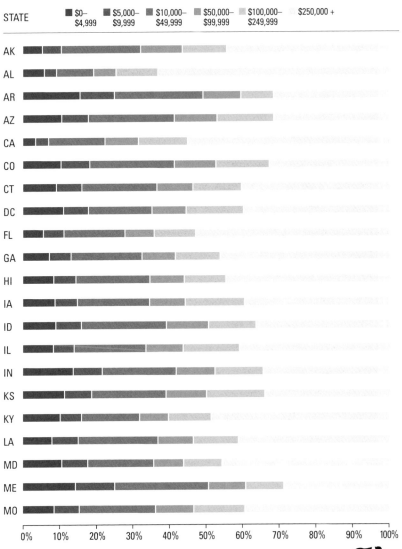

DISTRIBUTION OF PREMIUM BY PREMIUM RANGE BY STATE
(as of 9/14/2018) (continued)

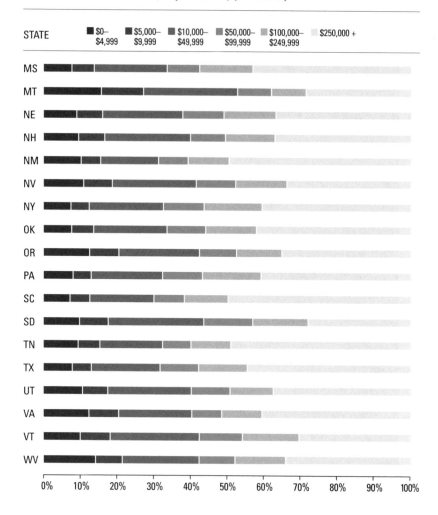

DISTRIBUTION OF PREMIUM BY PREMIUM RANGE — NATIONWIDE
(as of 9/14/2018)

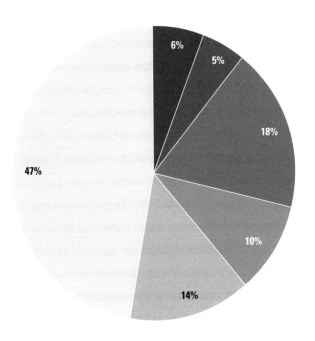

47%	$250,000 +	**10%**	$50,000–$99,999	**5%**	$5,000–$9,999
14%	$100,000–$249,999	**18%**	$10,000–$49,999	**6%**	$0–$4,999

DISTRIBUTION OF RISK COUNTS BY PREMIUM RANGE BY STATE
(as of 9/14/2018)

DISTRIBUTION OF RISK COUNTS BY PREMIUM RANGE BY STATE
(as of 9/14/2018) (continued)

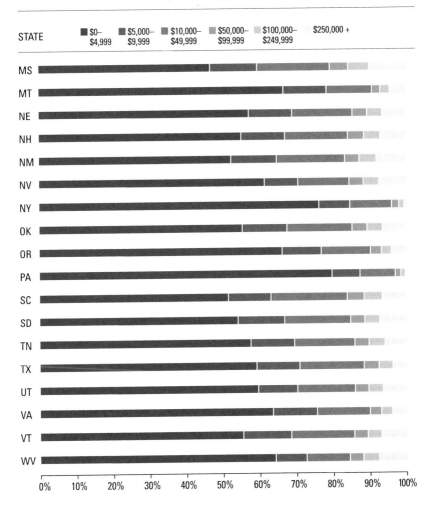

DISTRIBUTION OF RISK COUNTS BY PREMIUM RANGE — NATIONWIDE
(as of 9/14/2018)

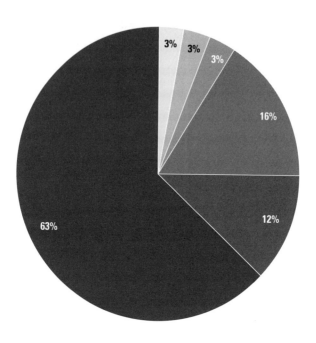

63%	$0–$4,999	**16%**	$10,000–$49,999	**3%**	$100,000–$249,999
12%	$5,000–$9,999	**3%**	$50,000–$99,999	**3%**	$250,000 +

MARKET CONCENTRATION OF WORKERS' COMPENSATION
INSURANCE CARRIERS *(as of 9/13/2018)*

State	2017	2015	2013	2011	2009	2007
Alabama	12.9%	11.3%	11.2%	12.3%	14.4%	18.2%
Alaska	34.1%	33.1%	31.3%	29.7%	28.3%	29.6%
Arizona	23.7%	25.1%	28.9%	30.6%	39.8%	55.2%
Arkansas	11.7%	10.4%	10.8%	11.8%	13.0%	17.7%
California	11.2%	13.3%	10.8%	12.9%	18.7%	26.4%
Colorado	57.7%	59.9%	58.8%	59.0%	53.4%	57.1%
Connecticut	15.4%	15.6%	16.8%	17.6%	18.5%	18.0%
Delaware	8.8%	8.4%	15.3%	21.0%	12.7%	16.3%
District of Columbia	18.8%	17.4%	20.3%	25.0%	23.3%	20.0%
Florida	11.1%	12.5%	13.6%	13.6%	14.5%	14.7%
Georgia	8.8%	8.6%	9.1%	9.4%	9.0%	11.9%
Hawaii	26.0%	27.7%	23.0%	17.3%	19.6%	21.4%
Idaho	59.6%	61.5%	60.3%	53.1%	56.5%	61.7%
Illinois	8.9%	9.4%	9.5%	9.9%	11.8%	14.1%
Indiana	9.0%	8.2%	9.5%	12.9%	15.9%	16.6%
Iowa	8.9%	8.5%	8.7%	9.2%	10.0%	10.1%
Kansas	12.5%	13.4%	11.1%	11.3%	12.6%	13.6%
Kentucky	31.1%	27.6%	29.3%	22.5%	23.0%	23.3%
Louisiana	25.3%	22.4%	22.8%	22.3%	24.3%	28.0%
Maine	67.4%	64.6%	62.6%	59.4%	62.2%	60.7%
Maryland	22.2%	23.4%	24.6%	23.1%	22.7%	27.7%
Massachusetts	13.2%	13.9%	13.9%	16.5%	16.0%	28.1%
Michigan	21.6%	17.9%	16.8%	17.5%	19.7%	20.2%
Minnesota	12.6%	11.5%	12.3%	12.8%	11.5%	11.1%

MARKET CONCENTRATION OF WORKERS' COMPENSATION
INSURANCE CARRIERS *(as of 9/13/2018) (continued)*

State	2017	2015	2013	2011	2009	2007
Mississippi	9.8%	9.3%	10.9%	11.0%	12.8%	17.2%
Missouri	25.3%	21.8%	20.2%	19.5%	14.8%	15.7%
Montana	59.9%	61.2%	60.9%	61.9%	63.6%	69.0%
Nebraska	12.8%	14.7%	14.8%	12.2%	10.7%	11.6%
Nevada	9.7%	9.3%	9.5%	14.4%	19.2%	22.6%
New Hampshire	13.7%	12.8%	13.9%	17.1%	22.0%	19.6%
New Jersey	19.3%	19.8%	23.7%	22.0%	22.3%	24.5%
New Mexico	37.3%	36.3%	34.1%	28.7%	29.7%	29.3%
New York	38.3%	44.1%	44.0%	36.0%	38.3%	40.0%
North Carolina	8.1%	8.5%	8.5%	8.9%	9.4%	11.7%
Oklahoma	30.5%	32.6%	30.5%	30.7%	32.6%	36.5%
Oregon	70.4%	69.2%	67.6%	61.2%	56.8%	61.4%
Pennsylvania	6.7%	7.9%	8.4%	7.4%	9.6%	13.8%
Rhode Island	56.1%	61.1%	61.3%	55.3%	58.7%	64.3%
South Carolina	8.7%	8.3%	9.3%	10.9%	11.1%	16.9%
South Dakota	15.2%	13.6%	11.9%	11.5%	11.5%	12.8%
Tennessee	11.5%	9.0%	9.6%	9.6%	11.1%	13.0%
Texas	42.3%	39.7%	38.6%	33.8%	29.0%	27.3%
Utah	50.5%	51.7%	50.9%	50.2%	49.9%	54.6%
Vermont	16.1%	14.7%	16.5%	20.9%	23.7%	20.8%
Virginia	9.3%	9.9%	10.3%	11.0%	12.3%	15.4%
West Virginia	52.3%	47.1%	52.7%	53.6%	76.5%	99.2%
Wisconsin	8.5%	10.9%	10.6%	10.0%	11.3%	12.0%
Total U.S.	**7.6%**	**7.8%**	**8.0%**	**8.3%**	**9.7%**	**11.6%**

MARKET CONCENTRATION OF WORKERS' COMPENSATION
INSURANCE CARRIERS *(as of 9/13/2018)* *(continued)*

STATE ■ Top 1 ■ Top 5 ■ Top 10 ■ Others

AL, AK, AZ, AR, CA, CO, CT, DE, DC, FL, GA, HI, ID, IL, IN, IA, KS, KY, LA, ME, MD, MA, MI, MN

0% 10% 20% 30% 40% 50% 60% 70% 80% 90% 100%

MARKET CONCENTRATION OF WORKERS' COMPENSATION INSURANCE CARRIERS *(as of 9/13/2018) (continued)*

WORKERS' COMPENSATION INSURANCE ADVOCATES FIND PASSION FOR COMPASSION

Claims advocacy is a "trend du jour" among workers' compensation insurance professionals, according to the responses of 700 participants in the Rising Workers' Compensation Benchmarking Study, released in August 2018. The study confirms that claims leaders know the value of advocacy, the process that is conducted with particular dignity, respect, and transparency in the settlement and administration of claims. Advocates feel that helping injured workers effectively factors into the recovery, health, and well-being of the worker — an obvious but worthy point to keep in mind.

A refreshed claims culture that makes access to benefits easy, while building trust and confidence, needs to be supported by broader organizational values and systems. Specifically, access to benefits should include ease of filing, ease in obtaining prescribed medications, access to medical specialists, and help in navigating healthcare delivery mazes. The Predictors of Worker Outcomes series from the Workers' Compensation Research Institute calls trust a key driver of favorable claims outcomes.

A culture of trust benefits the carriers as well as the workers. Clear and fast response to injured workers' plights pays off in the carrier's workers' satisfaction and invariably results in lower claims costs. A paradigm shift for workers' compensation professionals and institutions seems to be in the offing, as insurers move beyond performance metrics based primarily in cost containment to those based on high-quality outcomes.

Compassion for the injured party is especially helpful in attracting younger professionals, it has been opined. And the industry needs them badly, as more than half of insurance professionals are close to retirement.

FRAUD FOCUS: BOGUS REPORTING FLAGS

Where's Columbo when you need him?

Perhaps the legendary detective had this list in his raincoat in cases where workers' compensation fraud figured into a solution. Here we find clues that may result in discovering the crime that is insurance fraud in the workers' compensation field.

A claim usually does not pass the smell test when we find:

1. No witnesses to the purported incident.

2. The claimant refuses standard medical treatment.

3. The explanation is inconsistent.

4. The claimant has a history of compensation claims and/or changing jobs.

5. The incident happened just before the claimant was terminated.

6. The claimant has a side gig.

7. The claimant is found to be performing tasks or demonstrating abilities inconsistent with the injury.

8. The claimant hires an attorney, visits a chiropractor, and begins to accrue bills right away.

9. The claimant pushes for a fast settlement.

10. The claimant is strangely inaccessible.

NEW YORK STATE WORKERS' COMPENSATION BOARD
TO UPDATE MEDICAL FEE SCHEDULE

The New York State Workers' Compensation Board has proposed an increase in medical reimbursement to providers who treat workers' compensation patients. The proposed medical fee schedule includes an overall fee increase for all provider types, as well as additional increases for certain specialty provider groups. This proposed fee increase will potentially raise the number of authorized providers for injured workers.

The proposal includes updated current procedural technology (CPT) codes, increased conversion factors, and amended ground rules, which are available under the Medical Fee Schedules section on the board's website.

The New York State Workers' Compensation Fee Schedule has not changed substantially since 1996, and the new fees, it was argued, will ensure that providers in New York receive fair and reasonable reimbursement for prompt, quality treatment.

The Board is also committed to the adoption of a universal claim form to reduce paperwork in workers' compensation claims, development of an online medical portal and a push to broadly expand the types of providers authorized to treat injured workers.

The proposals are expected to have an enduring cost impact for providers.

EMPLOYER BREAKDOWN ~ *U.S. employer costs for employee compensation averaged $36.22 per hour worked in June 2018. Wages and salaries averaged $24.72 per hour worked and accounted for 68.3 percent of these costs, while benefit costs averaged $11.50 and accounted for the remaining 31.7 percent. Total employer compensation costs for private industry workers averaged $34.19 per hour worked. Total employer compensation costs for state and local government workers averaged $49.23 per hour worked.*

Source: U.S. Bureau of Labor Statistics

APPLIED PROTECTS THE
TITANS OF INDUSTRY.®

APPLIED
UNDERWRITERS

IT PAYS TO GET A QUOTE FROM APPLIED®

Accepting large workers' compensation risks. Most classes. All states, all areas, including New York City, Boston, and Chicago. Few capacity and concentration restrictions. Simplified financial structure covers all exposures.

EXPECT THE WINNING DEAL ON LARGE WORKERS' COMPENSATION.
Call (877) 234-4450 or visit auw.com to get a quote.

WORKERS' COMPENSATION PREMIUM RATE RANKING
(as of 8/10/2018)

2016 Ranking	2014 Ranking	State	Index Rate	Percent of study median	Effective Date
1	1	California	3.24	176%	January 1, 2016
2	3	New Jersey	2.92	158%	January 1, 2016
3	4	New York	2.83	154%	October 1, 2015
5	2	Connecticut	2.74	149%	January 1, 2016
5	5	Alaska	2.74	149%	January 1, 2016
6	9	Delaware	2.32	126%	December 1, 2015
8	6	Oklahoma	2.23	121%	January 1, 2016
8	7	Illinois	2.23	121%	January 1, 2015
9	20	Rhode Island	2.20	119%	August 1, 2014
10	10	Louisiana	2.11	115%	January 1, 2016
11	11	Montana	2.10	114%	July 1, 2015
12	23	Wisconsin	2.06	112%	October 1, 2015
14	8	Vermont	2.02	110%	April 1, 2015
14	13	Maine	2.02	110%	April 1, 2015
15	17	Washington	1.97	107%	January 1, 2016
17	27	Hawaii	1.96	107%	January 1, 2016
17	12	New Hampshire	1.96	106%	January 1, 2016
18	17	South Carolina	1.94	105%	September 1, 2015
20	21	Missouri	1.92	104%	January 1, 2016
20	20	New Mexico	1.92	104%	January 1, 2016
22	20	Minnesota	1.91	104%	January 1, 2016
22	27	North Carolina	1.91	103%	April 1, 2015
23	31	Wyoming	1.87	101%	January 1, 2016
24	24	Iowa	1.86	101%	January 1, 2016
25	29	Alabama	1.85	100%	March 1, 2015

WORKERS' COMPENSATION PREMIUM RATE RANKING
(as of 8/10/2018) (continued)

2016 Ranking	2014 Ranking	State	Index Rate	Percent of study median	Effective Date
26	17	Pennsylvania	1.84	100%	April 1, 2015
27	32	Georgia	1.80	98%	March 1, 2015
28	14	Idaho	1.79	97%	January 1, 2016
29	38	Mississippi	1.70	92%	March 1, 2015
30	22	Tennessee	1.68	91%	March 1, 2015
32	30	Nebraska	1.67	91%	February 1, 2015
32	25	South Dakota	1.67	91%	July 1, 2015
33	28	Florida	1.66	90%	January 1, 2016
34	34	Michigan	1.57	85%	January 1, 2015
35	41	Colorado	1.56	84%	January 1, 2016
36	40	Kentucky	1.52	82%	October 1, 2015
38	37	Arizona	1.50	82%	January 1, 2016
38	35	Maryland	1.50	82%	January 1, 2016
40	36	Texas	1.45	79%	July 1, 2015
40	33	Ohio	1.45	79%	July 1, 2015
41	39	Kansas	1.41	77%	January 1, 2016
42	45	District of Columbia	1.37	74%	November 1, 2015
43	46	Nevada	1.31	71%	March 1, 2015
44	48	Massachusetts	1.29	70%	April 1, 2014
45	43	Oregon	1.28	69%	January 1, 2016
46	45	Utah	1.27	69%	December 1, 2015
47	48	Virginia	1.24	67%	April 1, 2015
48	43	West Virginia	1.22	66%	November 1, 2015
49	49	Arkansas	1.06	57%	July 1, 2015
50	50	Indiana	1.05	57%	January 1, 2016
51	51	North Dakota	0.89	48%	July 1, 2015

RATIOS OF UNALLOCATED LOSS ADJUSTMENT EXPENSES
TO LOSSES BY STATE *(as of September 2017)*

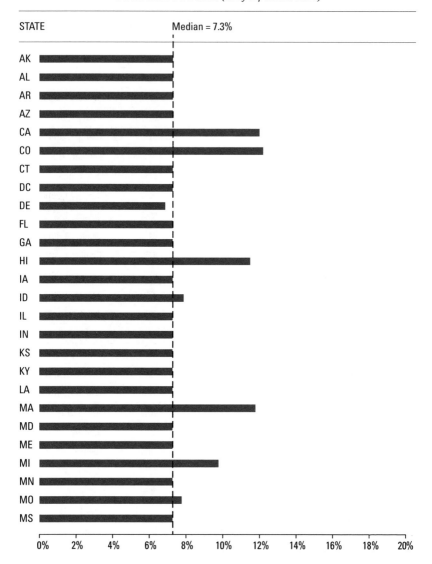

RATIOS OF UNALLOCATED LOSS ADJUSTMENT EXPENSES
TO LOSSES BY STATE *(as of September 2017) (continued)*

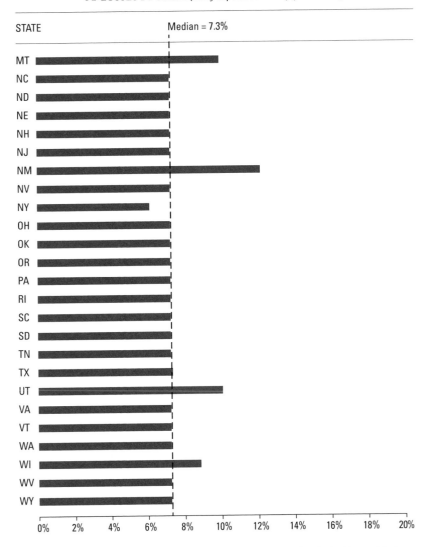

Note: States with the higher ratios of ULAE to loss typically have claims that are more complex, often involving cumulative trauma or permanent disability.

RESIDUAL MARKET MECHANISMS
(as of September 2016)

State	Competitive Fund	State Assigned Risk Mechanism	State Assigned Risk Plan Admin. by NCCI	Monopolistic State
Alabama		Y	Y	
Alaska		Y	Y	
Arizona		Y	Y	
Arkansas		Y	Y	
California	Y			
Colorado	Y			
Connecticut		Y	Y	
Delaware		Y		
District of Columbia		Y	Y	
Florida		Y		
Georgia		Y	Y	
Hawaii	Y			
Idaho		Y	Y	
Illinois		Y	Y	
Indiana		Y		
Iowa		Y	Y	
Kansas		Y	Y	
Kentucky	Y			
Louisiana	Y			
Maine	Y			
Maryland	Y			
Massachusetts		Y		
Michigan		Y		
Minnesota*		Y		
Mississippi		Y	Y	
Missouri*		Y		

RESIDUAL MARKET MECHANISMS
(as of September 2016) (continued)

State	Competitive Fund	State Assigned Risk Mechanism	State Assigned Risk Plan Admin. by NCCI	Monopolistic State
Montana	Y			
Nebraska		Y		
Nevada		Y	Y	
New Hampshire		Y	Y	
New Jersey		Y		
New Mexico*		Y	Y	
New York	Y			
North Carolina		Y		
North Dakota				Y
Ohio				Y
Oklahoma	Y			
Oregon*		Y	Y	
Pennsylvania		Y		
Rhode Island	Y			
South Carolina		Y	Y	
South Dakota		Y	Y	
Tennessee		Y	Y	
Texas	Y			
Utah	Y			
Vermont		Y	Y	
Virginia		Y	Y	
Washington				Y
West Virginia			Y	
Wisconsin		Y		
Wyoming				Y

* Competitive Fund does not serve as residual market mechanism.

2017 NONFATAL WORK INJURY AND ILLNESS RATE CASELOAD BY INDUSTRY TYPE

This chart shows the number, incidence rate, and median days away from work for nonfatal work injuries and illnesses by occupation group, within the private industry, state, and local government in 2017. The bubble size represents the number of cases in each group shown below:

1. Transportation & material moving
2. Production
3. Installation, maintenance, & repair
4. Construction and extraction
5. Protective service
6. Food preparation and serving related
7. Building & grounds cleaning & maintenance
8. Office and administrative support
9. Healthcare practitioners & technical
10. Healthcare support
11. Sales and related

12. Education, training, & library
13. Personal care & service
14. Management
15. Farming, fishing, & forestry
16. Community and social service
17. Business and financial operations
18. Arts, design, entertainment, sports, & media
19. Architecture & engineering
20. Life, physical, & social science
21. Computer & mathematical
22. Legal

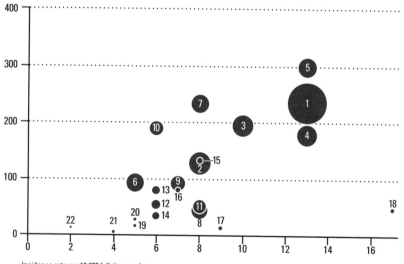

Incidence rate per 10,000 full-time workers.

EXPECT BIG THINGS®
FROM APPLIED UNDERWRITERS

Expect big things in workers' compensation. Most classes approved, nationwide. It pays to get a quote from Applied.®
For information call (877) 234-4450 or visit auw.com/us. Follow us at bigdoghq.com.

APPLIED®
UNDERWRITERS

SEXUAL HARASSMENT CASE LOADS INCREASE

Thirty-five percent of workers say they have experienced workplace harassment, and 50 percent of them believed it was due to their gender or sex. These are findings of a 2018 Hiscox Workplace Harassment Study, which surveyed 500 U.S. adults employed full time.

Of those who were harassed, 78 percent said it was perpetrated by a male, and 73 percent said their harasser was in a senior position. Respondents also reported harassment that was committed by women against men, by members of the same sex, and by non-company employees, such as customers or vendors. All these scenarios represent incidents in which a company could be subject to liability and financial loss if it has failed to appropriately protect its employees.

> **‟ The percentage of respondents who reported [harassment] was the same for companies with over 1,000 employees as is was for those with fewer than 200 employees. ”**

More than one in three employees surveyed said they had felt harassed, and 40 percent of those respondents said they never reported the harassment to company management or the police. The top reason cited for not reporting harassment was the fear that the allegations would create a hostile work environment (53 percent). The second reason was fear of retaliation, particularly termination. Of those who were harassed and did report it, 37 percent did not believe their employer handled the incident properly, and for women who reported harassment, this figure climbed to 49 percent. It's not just victims who don't report harassment: Forty-five percent of all respondents said they have witnessed harassment in the workplace, and 42 percent of them did not report it.

SEXUAL HARASSMENT CASE LOADS INCREASE *(continued)*

Companies of all sizes are subject to harassment claims. In fact, the percentage of respondents who indicated they had been harassed was the same at companies with fewer than 200 employees as it was at those with over 1,000 employees: 32 percent.

However, how companies approach harassment may vary. Fifty-four percent of respondents at companies with fewer than 200 employees said their firm does not offer anti-harassment training, compared to only 21 percent of those at firms with more than 1,000 employees. And only 39 percent of those at smaller firms reported that their company had implemented new workplace harassment policies within the past 12 months, versus 57 percent of their larger counterparts.

The good news is that the mindsets of employers and employees are changing. In an era of increased transparency and social movements such as #Me Too and Time's Up, employers are taking a more proactive approach to prevention. Eighty-five percent of respondents said they believed people were more likely to report incidents because of these social movements. Fifty-one percent of those surveyed said their companies had instituted new policies related to workplace harassment in the past 12 months.

Millennials tend to view this time of open discussion about workplace harassment to be more of the norm than their parents and grandparents do. Millennials were the most likely to say they were harassed — 46 percent — compared to 35 percent of Gen Xers. Millennials were also more likely to report harassment to company management or the police, with 76 percent of them having done so.

GOLDEN STATE – *California generates 20% of all workers' compensation premiums in the country but only represents 11% of the workforce in the U.S.*

Source: WCIRB

SEXUAL HARASSMENT CLAIMS: MORE EPLI THAN WORKERS' COMPENSATION

Sexual misconduct claims continue to dominate headlines. Marie-France Gelot, senior vice president and insurance and claims counsel in Lockton's Northeast operation, explains that this risk is typically covered under an employment practices liability insurance policy (EPLI) or a hybrid, private company directors, and officers liability (D&O) policy. Lockton is the world's largest privately held, independent insurance broker.

"As with any claim, the specific factual circumstances surrounding the matter will be critical in determining whether coverage is ultimately triggered," Gelot writes in her white paper "Sexual Harassment: Is Your Company Exposed?"

Many sexual harassment claims are filed under workers' compensation. The term "sexual harassment" is used widely today, but Gelot reminds companies that the Equal Employment Opportunity Commission (EEOC) has a specific legal definition for this phrase. She outlines the legal procedures for filing a sexual harassment claim under Title VII of the Civil Rights Act and explains specific claim scenarios where the line between insured versus uninsured acts can be confusing.

> ## *"*EPLI policies that do exclude bodily injury typically contain an exception for claims alleging emotional distress, mental anguish, and humiliation. *"*

Gelot offers an example in which a customer of a retail chain alleges being sexually harassed by a store employee while they were in the store and suffering damages as a result. This would likely constitute a covered claim under the company's EPLI policy, assuming that policy had third-party coverage. Many, but not all, EPLI policies cover claims brought by third parties, such as clients, customers, or vendors. Such a policy would provide defense costs coverage and indemnity coverage for the company and employee.

SEXUAL HARASSMENT CLAIMS: MORE EPLI THAN WORKERS' COMPENSATION
(continued)

Insurers also look at where the sexual harassment took place and if the employee was acting in the course and scope of their employment. For example, if an employee alleges that her manager sexually harassed her in a bar on a Saturday evening during a social event, the insurance carrier would most likely question whether the manager was on-the-job during the social event to determine whether coverage applied.

Employers should also be aware of frequent exclusions, such as the conduct exclusions for intentional acts and the bodily injury exclusion, which may broadly exclude coverage for assault and battery. Since the definition of battery is unwanted or unpermitted touching, this limits sexual harassment coverage to nonphysical sexual harassment only, even if that is not explicitly stated in the policy wording. However, EPLI policies that do exclude bodily injury typically contain an exception for claims alleging emotional distress, mental anguish, and humiliation.

Due to the coverage of recent sexual harassment cases, employees and employers are paying more attention to such claims. For now, corporations should examine their policies to ensure they have the right coverage. Gelot's white paper "Sexual Harassment: Is Your Company Exposed?" offers a sound understanding of the coverage needed should such a claim arise.

TRIPLE TIME – *A Workers' Compensation Research Institute (WCRI) study on the long-term use of opioids found that where workers had more than seven days of lost work time, longer-term opioid prescripts resulted in durations of temporary disability that were more triple those for claims with no opioid prescriptions.*

In contrast, a small number of opioid prescriptions, over a short period of time, did not lengthen temporary disability. The study analyzed data from 28 states between 2008 and 2013.

Source: WCRI

NCCI'S NUMBER ONE MISCLASSIFIED CODE IN 2017

 The National Council on Compensation Insurance (NCCI) conducts classification inspections in all NCCI states to ensure the appropriate and consistent application of their numeric classification system. The NCCI's Classification Inspection unit conducts physical inspections of policyholders' business operations to determine whether the classification code and/or governing code identified on each insurance policy accurately reflect the policyholders' current operation.

Each year, the company releases information on the top reclassified codes. All reclassification is based on inspection findings that were completed within the previous calendar year. The 2017 reclassification study, released in May 2018, reported the single-most reclassified code was 9015 — Building or Property Management — All Other Employees.

To understand why this code is highly reclassified, it's helpful to consider the following information related to Code 9015. The NCCI's Scopes* Manual includes the following for Code 9015:

- Applies to the care, custody, and maintenance of premises or facilities.

- Not applicable to an owner or lessee of a building who occupies the entire or principal portion of the premises for manufacturing or mercantile purposes.

- Includes doormen, security desk personnel, elevator operators, gatekeepers, and concierges.

- Separately rate maintenance or repair work at any location where the owner or lessee does not also perform janitorial services.

- Includes real estate management companies and real estate investment trusts.

NCCI'S NUMBER ONE MISCLASSIFIED CODE IN 2017 *(continued)*

Code 9015 operations were most commonly reclassified to:

Code 9012 Building or Property Management — Property Managers and Leasing Agents & Clerical, Salespersons: This applies to property managers, leasing agents, model home hosts, clerical staff, and outside salespersons employed by a building or property management company.

Code 8855 Banks and Trust Companies — All Employees, Salespersons, Drivers and Clerical: Applies to bank managers, tellers, loan officers, security personnel, armed and unarmed attendants, armored car operations, ushers, door attendants, and maintenance personnel for financial institutions that receive, lend, exchange, and safeguard money.

Code 8723 Insurance Companies — Including Clerical and Salespersons: Applies to insurance companies and their employees including office workers; customer service representatives; actuaries; inside claims adjusters/examiners/auditors; underwriters; professional support staff, such as lawyers; computer programmers; and agents, brokers, and ratemaking organizations.

Code 9060 — Club — Country, Golf, Fishing, or Yacht — All Employees & Clerical, Salespersons, Drivers: Employees working exclusively for a country club operation run by a hotel, resort, condominium, or other community association are assigned to Code 9060.

COMING UP SHORT – *The U.S. Department of Labor estimates the trucking industry is currently short 50,000 drivers on a base of 500,000 over-the-road truck drivers currently operating in the county. Experts attribute this to the Federal Hours-of-Service Rule, where drivers have to be off-duty for 10 hours after driving 11 hours, which results in a lot of hours away from home. Additionally, age-related restrictions, such as hazmat or long-haul trucking, where 25 years of age is a common insurance-based expectation, are believed to contribute to limiting growth.*

Source: Independent Agent

Expect big things in workers' compensation. Most classes approved, nationwide. It pays to get a quote from Applied.® For information call (877) 234-4450 or visit auw.com/us. Follow us at bigdoghq.com.

LOUISIANA LEADS IN WORKERS' COMPENSATION COSTS PER CLAIM

Workers' compensation total costs per claim in Louisiana were the highest in a recent study of 18 states conducted by the Worker's Compensation Research Institute (WCRI), an independent, non-profit research organization based in Cambridge, MA.

"Total costs per claim with more than seven days of lost time were higher in Louisiana than other study states* and also growing faster than many states," said Ramona Tanabe, WCRI's executive vice president and counsel.

The study, CompScope™ Benchmarks for Louisiana, 18th Edition, found the average total cost per workers' compensation claim in Louisiana have risen 4 to 10 percent per year since 2012 at claim maturities from 12 to 48 months. Increases occurred in all three major cost components of a workers' compensation claim: medical payments, indemnity benefits, and benefit delivery expenses.

Growth in both indemnity and medical costs drove the increase in Louisiana's average total cost per workers' compensation claim from 2011 to 2014 for claims at 36 months of experience, accounting for fairly similar shares of the growth, at 40 percent and 37 percent, respectively.

For the study, WCRI analyzed workers' compensation claims with experience through 2017 for injuries up to and including 2016, and, in some cases, a longer time frame was used to supply historical context.

The following are among the study's other findings:

- Higher and growing hospital outpatient payments per claim were an important driver of higher-than-typical medical payments per workers' compensation claim in Louisiana.

- Benefit delivery expenses in Louisiana were among the highest of the 18 states studied, notably for payments to defense attorneys.

- Duration of temporary disability accounted for part of the Louisiana trend in indemnity benefits per claim, increasing by about one week since 2011 at all claim maturities. Duration was 9 to 16 weeks longer in Louisiana than in other states with a wage-loss benefit system.

- Lump-sum settlements were also an important factor in indemnity costs per claim and cost growth.

* Other study states included were Arkansas, California, Florida, Georgia, Illinois, Indiana, Iowa, Kentucky, Louisiana, Massachusetts, Michigan, Minnesota, New Jersey, North Carolina, Pennsylvania, Texas, Virginia, and Wisconsin.

EXPERIENCE RATING DISTRIBUTION BY STATE

An experience modification (X-Mod) is used to adjust premium based on the employer's past loss experience. Ideally, it tailors insurance cost to the characteristics of the employer and motivates the employer to reduce losses. Although distributions of risk counts and premium by X-Mod range vary from state to state, and over time, they share some common characteristics. For example, both risk counts and premium are usually roughly bell shaped with the highest frequency slightly below 1. The curves are right-skewed, so more risks are concentrated below 1. More risks get small credit X-Mods. The relatively few risks at very high X-Mods help to "balance" the system. On the other hand, risk counts and premium have some different properties in distribution. For instance, curves of risk count have thinner tails than premium because risks with extreme X-Mods tend to be larger risks (with more credible experience) and so we see relatively more premium at the fringes than we do risks. Finally, note that extremely high X-Mods are pretty rare. In almost all states, for example, an X-Mod of 1.3 or above is very uncommon. See the next pages for examples.

"I was at work and tried to make it from the windowsill to the top of the refrigerator. How about you?"

EXPERIENCE RATING DISTRIBUTION BY STATE
(as of 9/1/2018) (continued)

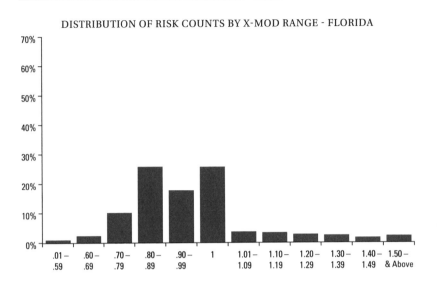

DISTRIBUTION OF RISK COUNTS BY X-MOD RANGE - FLORIDA

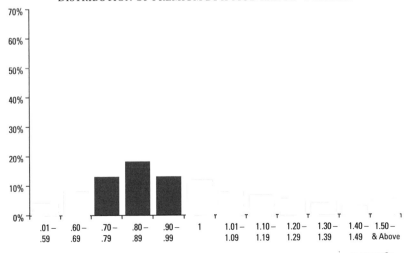

DISTRIBUTION OF PREMIUM BY X-MOD RANGE - FLORIDA

EXPERIENCE RATING DISTRIBUTION BY STATE
(as of 9/1/2018) (continued)

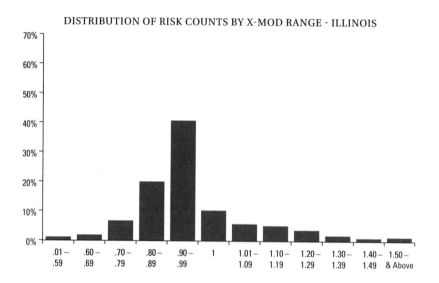

DISTRIBUTION OF RISK COUNTS BY X-MOD RANGE - ILLINOIS

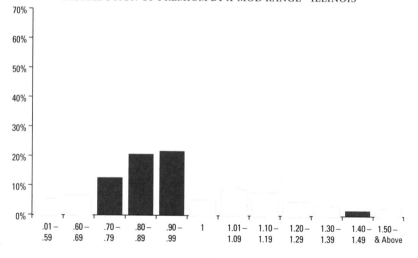

DISTRIBUTION OF PREMIUM BY X-MOD RANGE - ILLINOIS

EXPERIENCE RATING DISTRIBUTION BY STATE
(as of 9/1/2018) (continued)

DISTRIBUTION OF RISK COUNTS BY X-MOD RANGE - MARYLAND

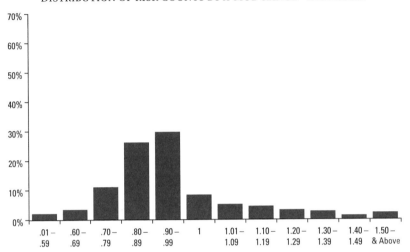

DISTRIBUTION OF PREMIUM BY X-MOD RANGE - MARYLAND

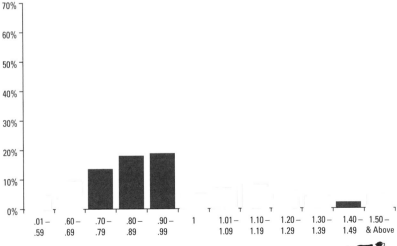

EXPERIENCE RATING DISTRIBUTION BY STATE
(as of 9/1/2018) (continued)

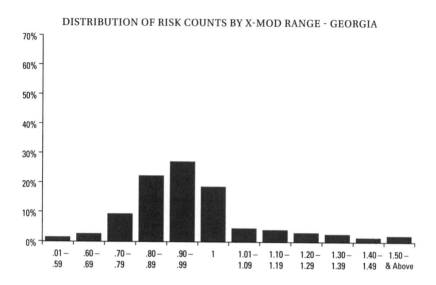

DISTRIBUTION OF RISK COUNTS BY X-MOD RANGE - GEORGIA

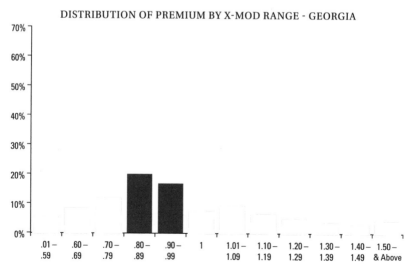

DISTRIBUTION OF PREMIUM BY X-MOD RANGE - GEORGIA

EXPERIENCE RATING DISTRIBUTION BY STATE
(as of 9/1/2018) (continued)

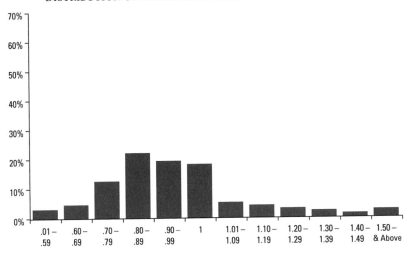

DISTRIBUTION OF RISK COUNTS BY X-MOD RANGE - ALABAMA

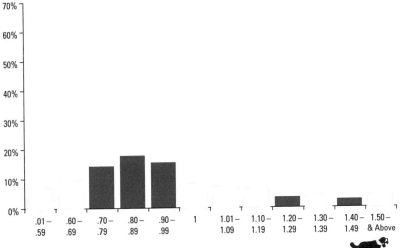

DISTRIBUTION OF PREMIUM BY X-MOD RANGE - ALABAMA

GENERAL LIABILITY CLAIMS IN FLORIDA

Workers' compensation immunity does not always preclude an employee's intentional tort claim. Florida's workers' compensation law is intended to provide a "quick and efficient delivery of disability and medical benefits to an injured worker and to facilitate the worker's return to gainful re-employment at a reasonable cost to the employer." Essentially, under a no-fault system, the employee gives up a right to a common-law action for negligence in exchange for strict liability and the rapid recovery of benefits.

> " Florida courts have identified there is a very narrow exception to the protection of workers' compensation immunity. "

For employees, workers' compensation is the exclusive remedy for "accidental injury or death arising out of work performed in the course and the scope of employment." While providing employees with benefits, the other side of this plan gives immunity from common-law negligence suits for employers.

Now, in some cases, Florida law allows employees to pursue a general liability claim against an employer and to sue an employer for an intentional tort.

Last year, the Florida Third District Court of Appeal allowed an employee to file a general negligence claim against his employer for a work-related injury because the employer had concluded that the injury was not incurred during the course of employment, and the employer had failed to submit a timely report of the injury to the carrier, which resulted in a denial of the claim. When the employee made a claim against the employer for general negligence, the employer asserted that it was entitled to immunity under the workers' compensation laws and filed a motion for summary judgment, which the trial court denied. On appeal, the appellate court affirmed, stating: "it would be inequitable for the employer, through its insurance carrier, to take the position that there were no work-related injuries and hence no workers' compensation coverage, and then later, when the employee brings a tort action against the employer, to assert as a defense at law that there was workers' compensation coverage entitling the employer to immunity from suit. As the employer may not separate itself from its compensation carrier's determination that the employee's injuries did not occur during the course and scope of employment, the employer is stopped from taking the totally inconsistent position that the injuries did occur during the course and scope of employment and claim worker's compensation immunity when sued in tort."

The point: an employee's general liability claim against an employer requires an investigation of the existence of workers' compensation insurance, whether a claim was made to the workers' compensation carrier and, if the claim was denied, whether the employer's representations to the workers' compensation carrier were inconsistent with those made during litigation.

The key elements of an intentional tort are these: the employer intended to injure the employee purposely, having engaged in conduct heedless of explicit warnings identifying the known danger, and leading to the injury; and the employer deliberately hid the danger so as to prevent the employee from exercising informed judgment.

> ## " Workers' compensation immunity does not always preclude an employee's intentional tort claim. "

One recent case, Gorham v. Zachry Industrial, Inc., specifically presents the standard for intentional tort as defined within the 2003 statute.

Mr. Gorham was working as a rigger on a Florida Power & Light power plant construction site when he was injured. On the day of the accident, the crew was attempting to lift and place a 9-ton wall. Two cranes were available to lift the large pre-fabricated wall into place. A tag line to keep the wall from swaying as the crane lifted it was attached to the wall, and because of the danger of swaying, attention to the wind speed was very important. On the day before the incident, the general foreman canceled the lift because the winds were over 20 miles per hour. The foreman testified that a lift would not occur if the winds exceeded 18 miles per hour. Mr. Gorham was injured when a wind gust blew the wall and he was dragged to the ground. He had contended that he relied upon his foreman to decide whether to proceed with setting the wall; based upon the foreman's decision to move forward, Gorham said he believed conditions were safe, even though it seemed to Mr. Gorham that the wind was blowing at approximately 30 mph.

In determining that summary judgment was appropriate, the court reasoned that there must be evidence that Zachry, through its foreman, knew that the wind speed was in excess of what was safe to perform the lift, and that lifting in that condition would with virtual certainty produce injury or death. While there was a dispute as to whether the foreman even took wind readings, taking the evidence in favor of Gorham as is appropriate in a party opposing summary judgment. It could be said that the foreman did not take the wind readings and allowed the lift to occur not knowing what the wind speed was; however, there was no evidence that such a lift would, with virtual certainty, cause injury. That afternoon the lift was performed without any injuries, even in increasing wind speeds. The court reasoned that the employer's conduct may have been grossly negligent, but it was not intentional.

More recently, the Third District affirmed summary judgments entered on behalf of two employing companies, in a case handled by Cole, Scott & Kissane, P.A., Vallejos v. Lan Cargo, S.A., 116 So.3d 545 (Fla.3d DCA 2013). In Vallejos, the Third District also examined the above-mentioned cases and, in affirming summary judgment for the statutory employers, reiterated the rule that "'virtually certain' means that a plaintiff must show that a given danger will result in an accident every — or almost every — time."

Based upon this case law, if an employee makes a claim for an intentional tort, an employer should mount an aggressive response as Florida courts have clearly identified that there is a very narrow exception to the protection of workers' compensation immunity.

CLAIM COUNT AND VOLUME OF PREMIUM (COMPARISON BY STATE)
(as of 9/1/2018)

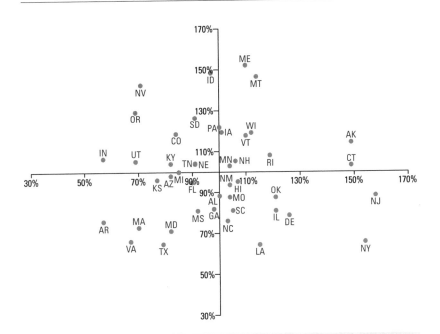

'SEXIST' OFFICE TEMPERATURE? ~ *A study released in August 2015 by Nature Climate Change found that indoor climates "are based on…a comfort level that was developed in the 1960s… based on the [metabolic rate] of an average male," which may be "intrinsically non-energy-efficient in providing comfort to female."*
In other words, women typically prefer warmer temperatures because their metabolic rates are slower; they're often cold when thermostats are set low to suit male metabolic levels. The study concludes that buildings should "reduce gender-discriminating bias in thermal comfort" because setting temperatures at slightly warmer levels can help combat global warming.

Source: Nature.com

COKE FLAT AS EEOC POPS $2.25 MILLION FINE

Coca-Cola Refreshments USA, Inc., a subsidiary of The Coca-Cola Company, and the Equal Employment Opportunity Commission (EEOC) reached a settlement agreement to resolve disability-related discrimination charges against the company. EEOC had issued fines against the beverage giant for leave policies affecting nine workers.

The deal continues the EEOC's crackdown on employer leave policies that the agency believes don't provide equal rights and opportunities to workers "on or returning from leave because a medical condition has left them temporarily unable to do their job." The agency has won settlements with many companies, but the agreement with Coca-Cola was reached through informal conciliation before a lawsuit was filed.

"This will improve policies and practices for individuals with disabilities and sets an example for many employers to follow," the agency's acting chair, Victoria A. Lipnic, said in a statement. "I commend Coca-Cola Refreshments USA and the EEOC staff in our Denver and Phoenix offices for bringing this matter to a successful resolution. I especially commend Coca-Cola Refreshments for agreeing to make the terms of this agreement public."

In addition to providing monetary relief for the nine workers, the $2.25 million will be used to provide annual financial support to nonprofit entities dedicated to helping workers with disabilities find and keep employment, the statement said. Coca-Cola Refreshments also agreed to improve the accommodations provided to employees returning to work after disability-related absences and will create "a dedicated accommodation and leave management team," the statement said.

Other companies that have entered agreements with the EEOC to resolve allegations of disability-related leave abuses include American Airlines and its regional carrier, Envoy Air, Lowe's Companies, and United Parcel Service.

WORKERS' COMPENSATION GLOSSARY OF TERMS

A

A.M. BEST COMPANY - Founded in 1899, A.M. Best Company is a full-service credit rating organization dedicated to serving the insurance industry. Policyholders refer to Best's ratings and analysis as a means of assessing the financial strength and creditworthiness of risk-bearing entities and investment vehicles.

ACCIDENT YEAR - The year in which a particular accident occurred.

ACCIDENT YEAR EXPERIENCE - Loss, adjusting, and claim count data for accidents occurring in a given accident year. Accident year experience changes as losses develop. Accident year losses are the losses that occurred during an accident year. Accident year losses, per year, change as claims develop. The ultimate accident year losses are known once all claims for that accident year are settled.

ACTUARY - An individual who projects a liability value using mathematical, accounting, and statistical analysis of past loss data.

ADJUDICATION - Resolving a controversy between parties by litigating the legal and/or factual issues. The court hearing usually pronounces a judgment based on the presented evidence.

ADJUSTER - Individual who settles a claim filed by an insured person. The adjuster evaluates the claim and determines the proceeds that may be payable for the claim.

ADJUSTMENT - The process of settling a claim. The settlement process includes evaluating the cause and amount of a loss, and determining the coverage and payment of any proceeds required under the insurance policy.

ADL - Activities of daily living.

ADMITTED ASSETS - The assets that are permitted by state insurance to determine the financial condition of an insurance company.

ADJUSTING AND OTHER EXPENSES (A&O) - The loss adjustment expenses not related to the defense, litigation or cost containment of a claim. This includes the cost of adjusters and the cost of inspectors and appraisers, while working in the capacity of an adjuster.

AGGREGATE LIMIT - The maximum amount the insurer will pay for all claims covered by a policy during that policy period.

ANNIVERSARY RATING DATE (ARD) - The date that determines the effective expense modification on a policy. It is usually the effective date of the policy (unless the rating board establishes a different date).

ANNUAL STATEMENT - The annual report an insurance company is required to file with the state insurance department in its domiciliary state.

ASSIGNED RISK - A policyholder who is unable to obtain voluntary insurance coverage and is assigned to the carrier of last resort, or to a pool of participating insurers.

ASSUME - The acceptance by a reinsurer (assuming company), of part or all of the written insurance transferred to it by the primary insurer or another reinsurer.

WORKERS' COMPENSATION GLOSSARY OF TERMS *(continued)*

ASSUMING COMPANY - The reinsurance company that accepts risk from a primary insurer or another reinsurer.

B

BASIC PREMIUM - A percentage of the standard premium used in calculating the premium of a retrospectively rated policy; the portion of the retrospective premium that is loaded to reflect a policy's expected overhead and profits and the net insurance charge.

BENEFITS - Monetary payments (and other services provided) by insurers to the insured party under the terms of an insurance policy.

BULK RESERVES - An additional amount added to reserves to account for claim development not included in the case reserves. Bulk reserves are not generally attributed to individual claims, but are an adjustment related to all outstanding claims.

C

CALENDAR YEAR LOSSES - The combined losses that were incurred during a calendar year. Calendar year losses include claim activity for the current-year claims and additional claim activity for prior-year claims that were incurred during a given calendar year.

CALENDAR YEAR PREMIUM - The combined premium written during a calendar year. Calendar year premium includes premium activity for the current calendar year only, regardless of the policy period.

CANCELLATION - Termination of an insurance policy before its expiration date.

This may be done by either the insurance company or the policyholder.

CARRIER OF LAST RESORT - An insurance company designated to accept a policyholder who has been refused coverage by all other insurance companies.

CEDE - The act of transferring all or part of the insurance written by an insurer (ceding company), to a reinsurance company.

CEDING COMPANY - The insurance company that transfers risk to a reinsurer. Also known as the cedent.

CERTIFICATE OF INSURANCE - A document issued by the insurance company that provides evidence of a policyholder's insurance coverage.

CLAIM - A request made by or on behalf of a claimant to an insurance company for payment of a loss covered by an insurance policy.

CLAIMANT - An individual who submits a claim to an insurance company for an incurred loss.

CLAIMS OUTSTANDING (OR CLAIMS PENDING) - The open claims a policyholder has at any given time.

CLAIMS RESERVES - The reserves attributed to an individual outstanding claim. Claims reserves are equal to total incurred payments less net payments (gross payments less subrogation).

CLAIM SEVERITY - Expected final cost per claim.

WORKERS' COMPENSATION GLOSSARY OF TERMS *(continued)*

CLASS CODE - An index by type of business operation used in grouping similar types of risks for rating purposes. Class codes are developed so that businesses with similar characteristics are charged similar rates.

COLLECTED PREMIUM - The amount of the premium that has been received as payment for an insurance policy.

COMBINED RATIO - The sum of the loss ratio and expense ratio. The combined ratio does not take into account or consider the investment returns on the premium received. It is common for the loss ratio to be an accident year ratio, while the expense ratio is calendar year, both expressed as ratios to calendar year premium.

COVERAGE A - Coverage through the part of a workers' compensation policy under which the insurance company promises to pay all compensation and benefits required of an insured employer under the workers' compensation act of the state (or states) listed on the policy.

COVERAGE B - Coverage through the part of a workers' compensation policy for situations in which an employee not covered under workers' compensation law could sue for injuries suffered under common-law liability.

D

DEATH BENEFITS - Indemnity benefits paid to the eligible survivor of a worker whose injuries resulted in death.

DEDUCTIBLE - A ground-up layer of loss retained by the policyholder. A workers' compensation insurance company is obligated to pay claims regardless of whether it is

successful in recovering the deductible.

DEPOSIT PREMIUM - The portion of the premium paid at the beginning of the policy that provides for future premium adjustments based on an estimate of the final premium.

DIVIDEND - A refund of the premium made to the policyholder by an insurance company out of its surplus or net worth, based on the insurance company's financial performance or insured's loss experience.

DATE OF INJURY (DOI) - The date an accident that causes an injury occurs.

E

EARNED PREMIUM - The premium applicable to the expired portion of the policy term for which the insurance was in effect.

EFFECTIVE DATE - The date that coverage begins on an insurance policy.

EMPLOYER'S FIRST REPORT OF INJURY - A report that employers are required to file with their workers' compensation carriers when one of their employees is injured on the job.

EMPLOYER'S LIABILITY - Catch-all term for coverages provided under a standard workers' compensation policy for common-law remedies not subject to workers' compensation.

ENDORSEMENT - An amendment attached to a policy modifying the terms of the insurance contract. The modification is only valid with the agreement of the insured, unless it is undoubtedly made solely for the benefit of the insured.

WORKERS' COMPENSATION GLOSSARY OF TERMS *(continued)*

ESTIMATED PREMIUM - A premium calculated using estimated payroll.

EXPENSE CONSTANT - A flat charge to cover the cost of issuing and servicing the policy.

EXPENSE RATIO - The percentage of premium used to pay for the acquisition, writing, and servicing of a policy. The expense ratio effectively reveals how much it actually costs the insurance company to write the premiums.

EXPERIENCE MODIFICATION FACTOR (X-MOD) - A factor that modifies the current policy premium to reflect the historical loss experience of a policyholder. The modifier increases or decreases the current premium depending on how the actual losses, for the past three years, compare with expected losses for the same amount of exposure in the same industry.

EXPIRATION DATE - The date coverage ends on an insurance policy.

EXPOSURE - Being subject to the possibility of a loss. For workers' compensation insurance, the typical exposure unit is payroll.

EXTRATERRITORIALITY - A provision in workers' compensation insurance law that extends protection to an employee that is injured in a state other than his state of hire.

F

FACULTATIVE REINSURANCE - Reinsurance that applies to part or all of some number of individual policies, giving the primary insurer and the reinsurer the faculty or option to accept or reject each policy to be reinsured.

FINAL PREMIUM - Final premium is calculated after a policy has expired and is calculated using actual payroll exposure.

FREQUENCY - The number of claims occurring over a period of time, relative to exposure. May be stated for an accident year or policy year, for an individual policy, a group of policies, or all policies.

G

GOVERNING CLASSIFICATION - A workers' compensation class code that has the most payroll exposure and generally describes the main business operation of the employer. The governing classification may not be a standard exception unless there are no class codes other than the standard exceptions.

H

HIPAA - Acronym for Health Information Portability and Accountability Act, a law established to protect the privacy of patients' medical records and health information.

I

IMPAIRMENT RATING - Established by a claimant's physician to quantify a physical disability, typically reflecting the percentage of the claimant's whole-body impairment. The impairment rating is determined by medical examinations using standard American Medical Association (AMA) guidelines. Individual states may have additional guidelines that supersede the AMA guidelines.

INCURRED BUT NOT REPORTED (IBNR) - Covered losses that occurred or have yet to

WORKERS' COMPENSATION GLOSSARY OF TERMS *(continued)*

develop, but have not yet been reported to the primary insurance company. A reserve is set up to account for this unknown liability to more accurately reflect expected losses.

INCURRED BUT UNPAID BENEFITS (IBUB) - The general liability accounts that reflect the reserves currently booked to pay any future liabilities on outstanding claims and IBNR claims.

IN-FORCE - Refers to the exposure for which an insurance company is providing insurance coverage on a given date.

INDEMNITY - Compensation for a loss. In workers' compensation, indemnity refers to compensation for lost time or reduced physical capacity as opposed to medical costs.

INDEMNITY CLAIM - A claim that includes payments and reserves for lost wages and medical expenses when an injured worker is out of work long enough to receive compensation for lost wages.

INDEPENDENT CONTRACTOR - An individual who does a job for another individual or company according to a contract, and is not an employee of the individual or company. An independent contractor typically has significantly more control (independence) over how and when the work is completed than an employee would have.

INDEPENDENT MEDICAL EXAMINATION (IME) - An examination of an injured worker by a physician selected by the insurance company. It is generally done to determine the appropriateness of a course of treatment, or to provide an evaluation of permanent impairment.

INFORMATION PAGE - The portion of a workers' compensation policy that describes a risk. It includes the insured's name and address, policy term, premium, and amount of coverage.

INSTALLMENT PREMIUM - Partial payment of a premium made by the policyholder for coverage on a term policy.

INSURANCE - The transfer of risk from one party (the insured) to another (the insurer) in which the insurer agrees to pay the insured (or their representative) an amount of money or service for losses sustained from an unexpected event, during a period of time for which the insured makes a premium payment to the insurer.

INSURANCE COMMISSIONER - The official of a state charged with the duty of enforcing its insurance laws. Also commonly called the superintendent of insurance or director of insurance.

INVESTMENT INCOME - Money earned from invested assets. An insurance company's invested assets usually include reserves and policyholder surplus.

L

LONG-TAIL LINE - A line of insurance coverage in which the occurrence and reporting of a loss and the payout of the claim is often spread out over a relatively long period of time. The length of time makes it difficult to determine the value of the claim when it is first reported.

WORKERS' COMPENSATION GLOSSARY OF TERMS *(continued)*

LOSS - The amount an insurer is obligated to pay because of an insured event. Also defined as an injury caused by an event covered by an insurance company.

LOSS ADJUSTMENT EXPENSES (LAE) - All of the costs associated with the settlement of a claim.

LOSS CONVERSION FACTOR (LCF) - A multiplier used in the calculation of the premium of a retrospectively rated policy, to include the cost of settling claims. Incurred losses are multiplied by the loss conversion factor to obtain an amount equal to the incurred losses plus estimated loss adjustment expenses.

LOSS COST MULTIPLIER - A factor an insurance company may file with the state insurance department to reflect the portion of the state's loss rates that the insurance company will charge for non-loss expenses.

LOSS RATIO - A ratio of losses plus loss adjustment expenses to earned premium. The loss ratio exhibits how much premium was actually used to cover losses and the cost to settle the losses. If loss adjustment expenses are not included, the ratio is more properly referred to as a pure loss ratio.

LOSS RUN - A report that lists the losses and expenses for claims filed on a policy over a given period of time. Also reports the premium earned for the period of time and the calculated loss ratio. Additionally, it provides a breakdown of losses by payments, reserves, and subrogation. In addition, losses are usually broken down further by type of loss. Only those expenses charged to a claim are listed on the loss run.

LOSSES INCURRED - An amount representing the losses paid plus the change in outstanding loss reserves within a given period of time. On an annual financial statement, the losses incurred are the losses paid during the year, plus the loss reserves at the end of the year, minus the loss reserves at the beginning of the year.

LOST TIME or TIME LOSS CLAIM - A claim in which an injured worker is unable to work for a period of time, as determined by a doctor. These claims typically involve the payment of disability benefits, in addition to medical costs and other expenses.

M

MANUAL PREMIUM - The premium before the experience modification and any premium discounts. Calculated by multiplying the exposure by the manual rate.

MANUAL RATE - The rate commonly used to calculate the premium on a policy. The manual rate is equal to the state rate or the loss rate multiplied by the appropriate loss cost multiplier filed with the state insurance commissioner.

MAXIMUM MEDICAL IMPROVEMENT (MMI) - The point at which an injured employee's condition is not expected to improve any further. Once a claimant obtains MMI, it is accepted that medical improvements in the future will be minimal.

MEDICAL CASE MANAGEMENT - Professional services provided for the evaluation, monitoring, and coordination of medical treatment for claims with specific diagnoses or requiring high-cost,

WORKERS' COMPENSATION GLOSSARY OF TERMS *(continued)*

extensive services.

MEDICAL ONLY CLAIM - A claim that includes payments only for medical expenses. It occurs when an injured worker was not out of work long enough to receive compensation for lost wages.

MINIMUM PREMIUM - The smallest possible premium charged for coverage during an annual period.

MODIFIED PREMIUM - The premium reflected after the adjustment for experience modification.

MONOPOLISTIC STATE FUND - State-operated insurance company that is the only provider of workers' compensation insurance in that state. With few exceptions, other insurance entities are not permitted to write workers' compensation insurance in these states. There are currently four monopolistic state funds: North Dakota, Ohio, Washington, and Wyoming.

MUTUAL INSURANCE COMPANY - A company owned and controlled by its policyholders. A mutual insurance company's surplus may be distributed to the policyholders in the form of dividends.

N

NATIONAL ASSOCIATION OF INSURANCE COMMISSIONERS (NAIC) - Composed of state insurance commissioners to promote uniformity by drafting regulations and model legislation. The NAIC has achieved considerable multistate uniformity through their annual statement, which insurance companies rely on for financial reporting.

NATIONAL COUNCIL ON COMPENSATION INSURANCE (NCCI) - An organization providing statistical services for insurance companies that write workers' compensation insurance in over thirty states. The NCCI collects statistics to establish rate structures in order to file rating plans with state insurance commissioners. The NCCI also maintains policy information and calculates X-Mods for these policies.

NEGLIGENCE - Failure to take the care that a reasonably prudent party usually takes, whether by omission or commission, in a given situation, resulting in harm to another.

NET - Calculated after the application of an offset. Premium, net of reinsurance, is direct premium plus assumed premium, less ceded premium. Losses, net of reinsurance, are direct losses plus assumed losses, less ceded losses.

NET INVESTMENT INCOME - The total earned from invested assets minus investment expenses. An insurance company's invested assets typically reflect reserves and policyholder surplus.

NET INVESTMENT INCOME RATIO - The ratio of net investment income to net earned premiums.

NEW BUSINESS - The written premium from a business that has not had a concurrent previous policy with the insurer.

NON-ADMITTED ASSETS - Any assets not considered by a state insurance department in determining the financial condition of an insurance company.

WORKERS' COMPENSATION GLOSSARY OF TERMS *(continued)*

NOT OTHERWISE CLASSIFIED (NOC) -
A class code term used to denote that a policyholder's operations cannot be classified more specifically.

O

OCCURRENCE - The result of an event that unexpectedly causes loss or damage.

OPERATING RATIO - The combined ratio minus the net investment income ratio.

OWNER-CONTROLLED INSURANCE PROGRAM (OCIP) - An insurance program usually written to cover large construction projects in which all labor performed under the contract is covered. The program usually includes insurance policies covering workers' compensation and general liability. Commonly called "wrap-up" policies.

P

PAID LOSSES - Total losses paid by an insurance company.

PAYMENT PLANS - Payment of a premium in periodic installments, usually monthly.

PAYROLL - Used to calculate the amount of the premium due on a workers' compensation insurance policy. Often used as the basis for projecting an employer's workers' compensation losses.

PAYROLL EXPOSURE - The amount of possible loss to which an employer's workers are subject, measured by payroll earned by covered workers. Used to calculate the amount of the premium due on a workers' compensation insurance policy.

PERMANENT DISABILITY RATING (PDR) -
A rating range from zero percent to 100 percent based on a number of factors (e.g., claimant's age, occupation, and the extent of permanent disability) and corresponds to a fixed number of weeks of indemnity compensation. Zero percent signifies no reduction of permanent earning capacity, while 100 percent represents permanent total disability. A rating between zero percent and 100 percent represents permanent partial disability. An injured worker with zero percent PDR would receive temporary indemnity compensation.

PERMANENT PARTIAL DISABILITY (PPD) - An injured worker that has a permanent impairment rating of less than 100 percent after the maximum medical improvement has been reached. Benefits for PPD are paid over a specified period of time, depending on the severity of the permanent impairment and the applicable state or federal compensation laws.

PERMANENT TOTAL DISABILITY (PTD) -
Refers to an injured worker whose injuries have rendered them permanently unable to perform the kind of work for which they are qualified, and who cannot perform other work that is reasonably available. In most, but not all cases, benefits for PTD are paid for the rest of the injured worker's life.

PHYSICIAN'S FIRST REPORT OF WORK INJURY - A report that a physician files with a workers' compensation carrier after an injured worker's initial examination by the physician after the accident.

POLICIES IN FORCE - The total number of policies that are active at any given point in time.

WORKERS' COMPENSATION GLOSSARY OF TERMS *(continued)*

POLICY PERIOD - The period of time during which a policy is effective or in force.

POLICY YEAR - The year in which the inception date of a policy falls.

POLICY YEAR EXPERIENCE - The matching of policy year losses with policy year premiums. Policy year experience changes as losses develop and the premium finalizes.

POLICY YEAR LOSSES - The total combined losses on policies incepting within a given policy year. Policy year losses for a given year change as claims develop. The ultimate policy year losses are known only once all claims that occurred during the given policy year are settled.

POLICY YEAR PREMIUM - The combined premium from policies incepting within a given policy year. Policy year premium for a given year may change as the premium adjusts in subsequent years. The ultimate policy year premium is known once all premium adjustments are finalized. Policy year premium includes the entire premium for a policy incepting in the policy year.

POLICYHOLDER ACQUISITION COSTS - The expenses incurred by an insurance company directly related to writing a policy.

POLICYHOLDER SURPLUS - The excess of an insurance company's assets above its liabilities. Shown as the balancing item on the statutory balance sheet.

PREFERRED PROVIDER ORGANIZATION (PPO) - A formally organized network of hospitals, physicians, and other healthcare providers. A PPO may negotiate directly for healthcare services at a lower price than would normally be charged.

PREMIUM - The amount paid by a policyholder to an insurance company in return for insurance coverage.

PREMIUM AUDIT - An examination of a policyholder's operations, books, and records by a premium specialist to determine the actual insurance exposure of the coverages provided.

PREMIUM REFUND - The amount of premium that has been collected over and above the final earned premium, and which is returned to the policyholder after a final audit.

PREMIUM RESERVES - There are two types: 1. A premium earned but not received (EBNR) is a premium due but not received by the end of the accounting period and 2. An unearned premium reserve (UEPR) is a premium paid for coverage beyond the end of the accounting period.

PREMIUM SPECIALIST - An individual who does premium audits for an insurance company. Also known as a premium auditor.

PREMIUM TAX - Payment made to a state or municipality by an insurance company, based on a written premium.

PROCEEDS - The benefits payable under an insurance policy.

PROFESSIONAL EMPLOYER ORGANIZATION (PEO) - A company providing outsourced insurance benefits and human resource consulting to other companies. The insurance benefits are provided as part of a group policy. Also known as employee leasing.

WORKERS' COMPENSATION GLOSSARY OF TERMS *(continued)*

PROSPECTIVE RATING - The determining of future premium rates based on the risk's historical payroll and loss experience over a specified past period of time.

R

RECOVERIES - Amounts received as reimbursement for paid losses. Recoveries include amounts from overpayments, subrogation, second injury funds, and deductibles.

REINSURANCE - An agreement whereby the reinsurer agrees to compensate the ceding company for all or part of the losses that the ceding company may experience under the policy or policies that it has issued.

REINSURED - An insurance company that has placed reinsurance risk with a reinsurer in the business of buying reinsurance. Also known as a ceding company.

REINSURER - An insurance company that assumes the liability of another by way of reinsurance.

REMOTE MONITORING - Process in which patients use a mobile medical device to perform routine tests (e.g., glucose meter reading or blood pressure monitoring) and send the data to a healthcare professional in real time.

RETROSPECTIVELY RATED POLICY - A policy in which the final premium is determined based on a formula using the current policy period's incurred losses. The formula elements and factors are included in the policy. Initially, the premium is estimated using expected losses. After policy expiration,

the premium is adjusted using actual losses. Retrospectively rated policies are similar to self-insurance in that some of the risk is retained by the policyholder. The retained risk under a retrospectively rated policy is limited.

RISK - Refers to the individual or organization insured and also the calculable uncertainty of financial loss.

RISK-BASED CAPITAL REQUIREMENTS (RBC) - Minimum capital standards that an insurance company must meet based on an assessment of the risk associated with the insurance company's operations.

RISK UNIT - An employee covered by workers' compensation insurance or an intrinsic item insured.

S

SCHEDULE CREDIT/DEBIT - A discount (or surcharge) available to policyholders, depending on individual state regulations. Schedule rating can provide a discount or surcharge based on the policyholder's risk characteristics, including but not limited to workplace safety programs, class peculiarities, and management cooperation with the insurance carrier.

SECOND INJURY FUND - Set up by states to encourage companies to hire workers who have been impaired by a prior workplace injury. After being hired by another company, when a worker has a second injury, the current company's insurance company is responsible for only the incremental costs due to the second injury by itself. Any increased cost due to worsened impact of the prior injury is covered by the second injury fund. Second

WORKERS' COMPENSATION GLOSSARY OF TERMS *(continued)*

injury funds are usually funded by general state revenues or by assessments on workers' compensation companies.

SELF-INSURANCE - Protecting against losses by setting aside a company's own money, rather than purchasing an insurance policy. By being self-insured, a company may save expenses that an insurance company charges for acquisition, premium tax, and general overhead. Typically, self-insured companies use a third-party administrator to administer their claims. Usually, they also purchase a special excess insurance policy to cover losses above their own retention.

SOLVENCY - The minimum standard of financial well-being for an insurance company, where assets exceed liabilities. When the solvency of an insurance company is threatened, state insurance laws require insurance regulators to step in and proceed with rehabilitation or liquidation.

STANDARD EXCEPTION - Refers to certain employee groups rated separately instead of being included under the main class code. In most states, the standard exceptions for workers' compensation are 8810 Clerical Office, 8742 Outside Sales, and 7380 Drivers, unless the main class code description states that one of these employee groups is included under the main class code.

STANDARD PREMIUM - The premium for a workers' compensation policy after adjustment for experience modification, safety credits/debits, schedule credits/debits, and association credits, but prior to adjustment for size and inclusion of the expense constant. The standard premium is often used in retrospective rating to calculate the basic premium, maximum, and minimum.

STATUTORY ACCOUNTING PRINCIPLES (SAP) - The rules of accounting and reporting required by state insurance law that must be followed by insurance companies in submitting their financial statements to state insurance departments.

STOP-LOSS PROVISION - A policy provision on a retrospectively rated policy that limits the loss amount for any individual claim that is included in calculating the retrospective premium. A stop-loss provision is an additional election, made by the policyholder, for which they are given a higher premium factor.

SUBROGATION - An insurance company's taking of legal action against a third party responsible for a loss to the insured to recover a claim which has been paid.

T

TELEHEALTH, TELEMEDICINE - The use of telecommunication and information technology to diagnose and treat patients from a distance. Includes videoconferencing, transmission of digital images, and remote monitoring.

TEMPORARY PARTIAL DISABILITY (TPD) - An injured worker's status prior to reaching maximum medical improvement, during which time they can perform some work, usually in a modified capacity or for fewer hours per day. Benefits for TPD are paid until the worker is released to full-duty work, or has reached maximum medical improvement.

WORKERS' COMPENSATION GLOSSARY OF TERMS *(continued)*

TEMPORARY TOTAL DISABILITY (TTD) - An injured worker's status prior to reaching maximum medical improvement, during which time they are unable to perform any work at all, as determined by a physician. Benefits for TTD are paid until the worker is released to return to work, or has reached maximum medical improvement.

TERM PAYROLL REPORT - A payroll report sent by a policyholder that describes the actual exposure that occurred during the policy period or term. The report is used to calculate final premium.

TERM POLICY - An insurance policy that is written with an established expiration date. Coverage continues only if the policy is renewed.

TERMS - The provisions described in an insurance policy.

THIRD-PARTY ADMINISTRATOR (TPA) - A company other than the provider of the insurance plan that is brought in to manage claims related to the insurance plan.

TOTAL INCURRED LOSS - An amount that represents the expected payout on a claim over the life of the claim. Incurred loss is equal to net paid losses (paid losses less recoveries) plus reserves.

TOTAL RESERVES - All total reserves of outstanding claims, whether known or unknown. Includes case reserves and bulk reserves and also reserves for loss adjustment expenses.

TRADE ASSOCIATION - A group of companies in a similar industry that is organized to obtain cost savings. A trade association may endorse an insurance company as its workers' compensation insurance carrier of choice in exchange for premium discounts for its members.

TREATY REINSURANCE - The reinsurance of some part of all the policies written by an insurance company under same broad conditions. Treaty reinsurance may be by quota share, where the insurance company and reinsurer share the risk based on a pro rata share agreement, or excess, where the reinsurer reimburses the insurance company for claims that exceed a predetermined loss amount. Compare this with facultative reinsurance.

U

ULTIMATE NET LOSS - The total payments resulting from a claim over the life of this claim, plus all related expenses, less recoveries and reinsurance. Total payment reflects that the loss has fully developed, and all loss payments are known.

UNDERWRITER - An individual who decides which applicants for insurance coverage are accepted or rejected, what coverage is provided, and what price to charge for this coverage.

UNDERWRITING PROFIT OR LOSS - An insurance company's profit or loss strictly from its insurance operations. This is in contrast to investment operations.

UNEARNED PREMIUM - The portion of the premium applicable to the unexpired period of the policy.

UTILIZATION REVIEW - The process that determines the medical necessity of services and procedures that have been submitted as necessary for a particular claimant.

WORKERS' COMPENSATION GLOSSARY OF TERMS *(continued)*

W

WORKERS' COMPENSATION INSURANCE -
Insurance coverage that is required by law to
cover employees in cases of injury or death
due to an occupational disease or accident,
regardless of the employer's negligence.

**WORKERS' COMPENSATION UNIT
REPORT** - A statistical representation that
provides information about payroll, the
premium, and losses for a specific policy
and state.

WRITTEN PREMIUM - Refers to the entire
amount of the premium written during a
described period, regardless of which portions
have and have not been earned.

SOURCES

SOURCES *(continued)*

SOURCES *(continued)*

SOLUTIONS

CROSSWORD PUZZLE

Across:
4. AGGREGATE
5. LOSSRESERVE
6. RV (RATE)
9. CEDED
11. POOL
12. LAPSE
13. SIU
14. NONADMITTED
16. CAPTIVE
18. DEDUCTIBLE
17. SUBROGATION

Down:
1. ACTUARY
2. PROVISION
3. SECOND
8. LOST
10. COMMISSIONS
15. DIVIDEND
16. COMMIS

SOLUTIONS (*continued*)

WORD SEARCH

C	D	E	O	P	K	T	R	R	A	C	D	C	R	E
O	F	G	J	V	C	S	A	I	I	Z	I	O	A	T
V	D	A	E	U	E	T	I	M	S	H	S	D	H	A
E	T	R	C	M	I	R	E	R	E	K	A	E	N	R
R	L	E	O	N	P	D	E	Y	I	Q	B	O	M	E
A	V	V	G	C	I	L	Y	X	J	T	I	F	C	S
G	C	O	K	P	A	V	O	L	E	T	L	B	X	A
E	R	C	E	C	K	A	B	Y	A	R	I	U	A	B
R	J	Y	M	I	A	L	C	C	E	Y	T	V	M	H
O	H	T	F	O	R	M	I	A	E	R	Y	I	A	U
H	G	L	A	H	P	F	K	C	B	Q	L	N	O	Y
K	W	A	S	S	I	G	N	E	D	R	I	S	K	N
S	I	U	Z	S	N	O	I	T	A	L	U	G	E	R
S	O	S	S	E	X	P	O	S	U	R	E	C	B	B
A	Z	A	A	M	M	T	A	U	V	F	A	I	B	V
L	L	C	A	P	O	U	F	D	P	R	S	J	Y	S
C	F	T	R	A	Y	X	K	U	U	B	H	A	N	I

SOLUTIONS *(continued)*

ANAGRAMS SOLUTIONS

1. EAGLE EYE WAVER GAWK
   Average Weekly Wage

2. DEBIT INTENSIFY MEN
   Indemnity Benefits

3. FOREFRONT SPIRIT JURY
   First Report of Injury

4. BOTANICAL FIVE NOTES
   Vocational Benefits

5. ADVISE SOUL SHORTLY
   Valued Loss History

6. IMPROVIDENT DECAL WORKER
   Medical Provider Network

7. PORTLY MICE
   Policy Term

8. GET PENNANT INDEED
   Independent Agent

9. AC/DC METAL EPIC
   Accepted Claim

10. LEASED COLD
    Closed deal

SPOT THE PHONY ANSWER

"Take a Knee" is the phony. While the nurse's original claim was denied, an overruling decision by the court of appeals noted "the employer takes the worker as the worker is found, that is, with all the physical strengths and weaknesses the worker brings to the job. If a lame worker suffers an employment fall and is injured, the injury is said to arise out of and in the course of employment under the same test applied for workers not lame. By the same token, if an awkward worker stumbles and falls, the rule is the same as if the worker were agile."

NOTES

NOTES

NOTES

NOTES

NOTES

NOTES

We wrote the book on Workers' Compensation.™

**IT PAYS TO GET A QUOTE
FROM APPLIED®**

(877) 234-4450

or

submissions@auw.com